THE CASE FOR
ORTHODOX THEOLOGY

Publisher's Note

THIS BOOK is one of a series of three, written at the request of the publisher: *The Case for Orthodox Theology,* by Edward John Carnell; *The Case for Theology in Liberal Perspective,* by L. Harold DeWolf; and *The Case for a New Reformation Theology,* by William Hordern. They are intended to provide for the lay person, student, teacher, and minister a clear statement of three contemporary theological viewpoints by convinced adherents to these positions.

Each author began with the same description of the purpose of the series and was provided perfect freedom to state his case. No one of the authors, moreover, knew the identity of the other two contributors until after manuscripts were completed; and at no time did any of the three have access to the manuscripts of the others.

THE CASE FOR ORTHODOX THEOLOGY

by
Edward John Carnell

Philadelphia
THE WESTMINSTER PRESS

Carnell, Edward John, 1919–
   The case for orthodox theology.
Philadelphia, Westminster Press [1959]
   149 p.   22 cm.
   Includes bibliography.

   1. Christianity — Essence, genius, nature.   1. Title.

BR121.2.C3   230   59–5515‡
Library of Congress

*To my father and mother
who lived as well as preached
the orthodox faith*

Acknowledgments

Grateful acknowledgment is hereby made to the following, who have granted permission to quote from copyrighted publications: Baker Book House, for quotations from James Buchanan, *The Doctrine of Justification.*

Wm. B. Eerdmans Publishing Company, for quotations from Herman Bavinck, *Our Reasonable Faith;* John Calvin, *Commentary on Genesis;* Charles Hodge, *Commentary on the Epistle to the Romans;* Abraham Kuyper, *Principles of Sacred Theology* and *The Work of the Holy Spirit;* James Orr, *God's Image in Man* and *Revelation and Inspiration.*

H. Richard Niebuhr, for quotations from *The Social Sources of Denominationalism.*

The Presbyterian and Reformed Publishing Company, for quotations from B. B. Warfield, *Biblical and Theological Studies* and *The Inspiration and Authority of the Bible.*

Zondervan Publishing House, for quotations from Patrick Fairbairn, *The Revelation of Law in Scripture; Fairbairn's Imperial Standard Bible Encyclopedia;* J. C. Ryle, *Expository Thoughts on the Gospels: St. John,* Vol. II; Wm. G. T. Shedd, *Dogmatic Theology.*

Scripture quotations are from the Revised Standard Version of the Bible, copyrighted 1946 and 1952, and are used by permission of the copyright owners, the National Council of the Churches of Christ in the U.S.A.

Contents

Preface

ORTHODOXY *is that branch of Christendom which limits the ground of religious authority to the Bible.* No other rule of faith and practice is acknowledged. Orthodoxy is friendly toward any effort that looks to Scripture; it is unfriendly toward any that does not.

The purpose of this book is to state and defend the orthodox faith. Statement and defense, however, are not the same thing. Statement draws on theology; defense draws on apologetics.

The theology of orthodoxy looks to a long tradition of exegetical and confessional labor. I have made a heavy draft on this tradition. There is no other way, short of outright plagiarism, to bring orthodoxy's case before the modern mind. Most of my citations, however, are from Reformed sources. This reflects a limitation in my own background. It also reflects my conviction that the Reformed faith, despite its shortcomings, is the most consistent expression of orthodoxy. But I trust that this limitation will not seriously depress the value of my work. I have tried to deal with issues that unite, rather than divide, the church. Moreover, a terminal bibliography of general theological sources has been added.

Orthodoxy has no official or traditional apologetics. Since attacks on the faith are being constantly revised, each generation must formulate its own defensive strategies. It should be said, therefore, that *I alone* am responsible for the apologetical arguments in this book. A poor showing at this point does not imply a deficiency in classical orthodoxy. It implies only that I am a poor apologist.

13

I have tried to be prophetic in my approach. This has not been easy, for a prophet must speak against, as well as to, his people. Original sin tinctures the claims of orthodoxy, and it is the duty of the prophet to point this out. But in doing so, the prophet is bound to incur censure from those who are too sure of their own perfection. I do not shrink from this threat.

Since original sin is also at work in the life of the prophet, I have doubtless misrepresented truth at points. This is not a happy admission, but I long ago despaired of infallibility. Convictions may prompt one to speak, but they do not notarize the truth of one's judgments. I therefore commit this book to the general public with the solemn words of John Gill before me: " If I have wrote any thing contrary to the divine perfections, or what may reflect any dishonour on the dear name of Jesus, or be any way injurious to the truth as it is in him, or be detrimental to the interest of pure and undefiled religion, I do most humbly intreat forgiveness at the hands of God."

E. J. C.

Fuller Theological Seminary
Pasadena, California

I.

Foundations

GREEK philosophy had no devotional impulse. The God of Plato served as a principle of form and order, but he did not inspire worship. Since the world occupied an inferior place in the spectrum of being, God could not enter time without defilement. God entrusted the grosser work of creation to the Demiurge.

Aristotle made things even worse. The God of Aristotle was so transcendent that he did not even know the world existed. If God knew the world — so Aristotle presumed — he would know change; and any change in God would be a change for the worse. Hence, the God of Aristotle did not exercise providence over the world. He was absorbed in eternal thought.

Christianity offended Greek wisdom by asserting that God mediated his will through the particularity of time. God entered history and performed redemptive events on behalf of his covenant children. Love took primacy over reason. This was a unique religious claim. "For ask now of the days that are past, which were before you, since the day that God created man upon the earth, and ask from one end of heaven to the other, whether such a great thing as this has ever happened or was ever heard of. Did any people ever hear the voice of a god speaking out of the midst of the fire, as you have heard, and still live? Or has any god ever attempted to go and take a nation for himself from the midst of another nation, by trials, by signs, by wonders, and by war, by a mighty hand and an outstretched arm, and by great terrors, according to all that the Lord your God did for you in Egypt before your eyes? To you it was shown, that you

might know that the Lord is God; there is no other besides him."
(Deut. 4:32-35.)

The Greek effort was ironic, for God and man were separated
out of a resolute effort to unite them. To ensure an affinity between
God and man, the Greeks defined God after man's highest virtue —
the faculty of reason. In this way theology became an extension of
anthropology. Since the real man is the rational man, the real God
is the rational God; God and man share the claims of universal
reason.

It never occurred to the Greeks that the rational man is subject
to the interests of the vital man. This oversight inspired the optimism that prejudice was confined to the market place. The groves of
Academe carried on an impartial dialogue with eternity. But dialogue it was, not worship. And it was not worship because God was
only a heavenly philosopher. God provoked a sense of rational awe,
but not a sense of moral unworthiness. God was too distant to be
comprehended, too proximate to be worshiped.

Socrates along the River Styx, asking questions but never learning — this is the final word from Greek philosophy. Since reason
is confined to universals, the species enjoys an essential advantage
over the particular. The God of Socrates knew *mankind,* but not
Socrates. Only love can grasp the particular. But the God of the
Greeks was thought, not love. The Greeks had no conception of the
heights of God because they had no conception of the state from
which man had fallen. They therefore had no remedy to restore man
to perfection.

1. *The Covenant with Abraham*

The Children of Israel had no occasion to indulge Greek vanity.
Grinding under Egyptian tyranny, they grieved in body and soul.
Pride had run its course. No consolation could be drawn from the
claims of universal reason. If deliverance were to come, it would
come from resources beyond man; and it would come by grace and
not by merit.

It was against this backdrop of total ethnic bondage that God
called a people and made a nation of them. A despair of self led to

hope in God. " And the people of Israel groaned under their bond-age, and cried out for help, and their cry under bondage came up to God. And God heard their groaning." (Ex. 2:23-24.)

The national life of the Jews began with the rite of the Passover. " You shall observe this rite as an ordinance for you and for your sons for ever. And when you come to the land which the Lord will give you, as he has promised, you shall keep this service. And when your children say to you, ' What do you mean by this service? ' you shall say, ' It is the sacrifice of the Lord's passover, for he passed over the houses of the people of Israel in Egypt, when he slew the Egyptians but spared our houses.' And the people bowed their heads and worshiped." (Ch. 12:24-27.) The Passover became a sacramental link in the generations of pious Jews until the coming of Jesus Christ. Jewish history was meaningful because God revealed him-self through deeds of kindness. The God of Abraham confounded human wisdom by extending his love to the unlovely. The Greeks did not share in this redemptive order. Greek history had no teleology.

Since there was nothing in the Children of Israel that gave them a meritorious advantage over others, the exodus defied the neat lines of general wisdom. The exodus traced to divine election. " For you are a people holy to the Lord your God; the Lord your God has chosen you to be a people for his own possession, out of all the peoples that are on the face of the earth. It was not because you were more in number than any other people that the Lord set his love upon you and chose you, for you were the fewest of all peoples; but it is because the Lord loves you, and is keeping the oath which he swore to your fathers, that the Lord has brought you out with a mighty hand, and redeemed you from the house of bondage, from the hand of Pharaoh king of Egypt." (Deut. 7:6-8.) God is a per-son, not a metaphysical principle. He freely does the whole counsel of his will. Hence, any effort to construct a " great chain of being " is self-defeating. The *telos* of the universe traces to the mind of God. Until God speaks, this *telos* remains inaccessible.

Since the exodus typifies the deliverance of a Christian through the cross of Christ, it is the greatest redemptive event in the Old

Testament. But anteceding the exodus is the day when "the Lord made a covenant with Abram" (Gen. 15:18). The Children of Israel cried unto God, and "God remembered his covenant with Abraham, with Isaac, and with Jacob" (Ex. 2:24). Deliverance from Egypt was the first blessing in the new covenant relation.

When Abraham was called a "friend of God," the contrast between Greek and Biblical thought became complete. The God of Abraham set his love on an individual. "The world did not know God through wisdom." (I Cor. 1:21.) God revealed himself through gracious words and kindly acts. And it was to Abraham and his posterity, not to the Greeks, that the revelation came. "The thing that stands in the foreground of that history is this: not what Abraham knows about God and does for God, but what God gives to Abraham. First, it is God who seeks Abraham out, and calls him, and leads him to Canaan. Second, it is he who promises that he will be a God to him and to his seed. Third, God promises Abraham that, all expectations to the contrary, he will have a posterity, will become the father of a great nation, and that this nation will have Canaan as its inheritance. Fourth, God says that in his posterity Abraham will be a blessing to all the nations of the earth. And, fifth, God draws up this promise in the pledge of a covenant, seals it with the sign of circumcision, and, after Abraham's trial of faith, confirms it with an oath." [1]

Abraham is a blessing to all nations because Jesus Christ is the true offspring of Abraham. There is one covenant; it unites both economies in the Bible. "Now the promises were made to Abraham and to his offspring. It does not say, 'And to offsprings,' referring to many; but, referring to one, 'And to your offspring,' which is Christ." (Gal. 3:16.) The just shall live by faith. And it is not important when or where this faith is expressed. God resists the proud, but he gives grace to the humble. All who repent of their sins — whether Jews or Greeks — share in the blessings of the Abrahamic covenant. "So then, those who are men of faith are blessed with Abraham who had faith." (V. 9.)

The severity of Old Testament law in no way nullifies the plenitude of grace in the Abrahamic covenant, for the law was *never* designed as a means of justification. Law unmasks pride and self-sufficiency; it prepares for grace by revealing sin. "Law came in, to increase the trespass; but where sin increased, grace abounded all the more." (Rom. 5:20.)

As the Children of Israel receded from the historical locus of the exodus, they became increasingly tempted to identify their prosperity with either pluck or virtue. Moses anticipated this threat. "Beware lest you say in your heart, 'My power and the might of my hand have gotten me this wealth.' You shall remember the Lord your God, for it is he who gives you power to get wealth; that he may confirm his covenant which he swore to your fathers, as at this day." (Deut. 8:17-18.)

The law became a terror because the people trusted in themselves. If this erosion of faith had continued through the centuries, the covenantal line would have vanished before the coming of Christ. "Without the law, so to speak, the promise and its fulfillment would have come to nothing. Then Israel would quickly have fallen back into paganism, and would have lost both her revelation of God with its promise and her own religion and her place among the nations. But now the law has fenced Israel in, segregated her, maintained her in isolation, guarded her against dissolution, and has thus created an area and defined a sphere in which God could preserve his promise purely, give it wider scope, develop it, increase it, and bring it always closer to its fulfillment. The law was serviceable to the fulfillment of the promise. It placed everybody under the wrath of God and under the sentence of death, it comprehended everybody within the pale of sin, in order that the promise, given to Abraham and fulfilled in Christ, should be given to all believers and that these all should attain to the inheritance as children (Gal. 3:21 and ch. 4:7)."[2]

2. Prophets and Apostles

General history is never normative; nor is it necessary that it should be. A historian believes that Napoleon attacked Russia to appease his will-to-power; but whether this was the only motive, or even the strongest, cannot be demonstrated.

But redemptive history *must* be normative. Otherwise faith does not believe on the sheer testimony of God's Word. Since the redemptive events answered to the divine interests, only God could reveal their meaning. By no scientific or philosophic effort could general wisdom discover how Abraham would become a blessing to all nations. An obscure individual leaves an obscure land — but what of it? What expectations could be grounded on this commonplace event? Would Abraham's children become accomplished musicians? Would they contribute to international law? Conjecture is futile because the Abrahamic covenant was initiated by God. The details of the covenant were not even revealed to Abraham. God simply gave his Word. But to Abraham, a man of faith, this was enough.

Inspired prophets stood between the redemptive events and the Old Testament community. " No prophecy of scripture is a matter of one's own interpretation, because no prophecy ever came by the impulse of man, but men moved by the Holy Spirit spoke from God." (II Peter 1:20-21.) The prophets looked in two directions, backward and forward — backward to the redemptive events and forward to the inexpressible gift of Jesus Christ. " God's saving acts in Israel — his dealings in grace with the nation and its fathers — stood behind the prophets' message, and formed the basis of their knowledge of God and confidence in him." [3]

The Old Testament disclosed the terms of the covenant, but the disclosure was veiled under temporal blessings. " When he admitted Abraham, Isaac, and Jacob, with their posterity, to the hope of immortality, he promised them the Land of Canaan as their inheritance; not that their hopes might terminate in that land, but that in the prospect of it they might exercise and confirm themselves in the hope of that true inheritance which was not yet visible." [4]

The apostles stood between the redemptive events and the New Testament community. They rendered a normative interpretation of Christ's Messianic office as Son of Man and Son of God. This interpretation forms the theology of the Christian church.

The marks of an apostle were to be with Jesus from the beginning, to be appointed by Jesus, and to perform signs and wonders. "The apostles, therefore, were the immediate messengers of Jesus Christ, sent to declare his gospel, endued with the Holy Spirit, rendering them infallible as teachers, and investing them with miraculous powers, and clothed with peculiar prerogatives in the organization and government of the church." [5] The apostles did not develop a cultic gnosis; they did not contrive a metaphysic of being. They had one message: God made a covenant with Abraham, and Jesus Christ is the blessing of this covenant. "That which was from the beginning, which we have heard, which we have seen with our eyes, which we have looked upon and touched with our hands, concerning the word of life — the life was made manifest, and we saw it, and testify to it, and proclaim to you the eternal life which was with the Father and was made manifest to us." (I John 1:1-2.) Since the testimony of the apostles is normative, no generation has a final advantage over any other.

3. *The Church*

The church is a fellowship of all who share in the blessings of the Abrahamic covenant. The *time* of appropriation is circumstantial. The fellowship in the Old Testament was the bud; the fellowship in the New Testament, the flower. The two phases differ in glory but not in substance. The church is one because the prophets and apostles spoke one Word. The church is the seed of Abraham. "So then you are no longer strangers and sojourners, but you are fellow citizens with the saints and members of the household of God, built upon the foundation of the apostles and prophets, Christ Jesus himself being the chief cornerstone, in whom the whole structure is joined together and grows into a holy temple in the Lord." (Eph. 2:19-21.)

But the church is also an organization. The reason for this is clear. The church is formed of sinners, and sinners are motivated by interest as well as by grace. Therefore, unless Christian behavior is kept decent and orderly, the fellowship will be frustrated. It was with this in view that the apostles appointed officers. Ecclesiastical rule is among the gifts of the Holy Spirit.

But the exact limits of ecclesiastical rule are nowhere defined. The apostles did *not* legislate a specific polity on the church. Nor is this to be construed as an oversight, for a precise theological principle was at work. Since love is higher than law, the organization is a servant of the fellowship. If love were perfect, law would be transcended. Christ alone would rule the church. Laws are made for the unrighteous.

Here is the final norm: *Polity is good or bad to the degree that it promotes or hinders the fellowship.* Too little rule invites anarchy; too much rule invites tyranny. In either case the fellowship is frustrated. The only escape from these perils is a dedication that looks to the God of the covenant, not to human wisdom, for the final defeat of evil.

Collateral Reading

1. The general purpose of law in Scripture: Calvin, *Institutes,* II. vii.

2. How the Old Testament prepares for the New Testament: Barrows, E. P., "Antecedents of Gospel History," in *Bibliotheca Sacra,* Vol. XXVII (1870), pp. 721–740.

II.

Faith

Faith is the capacity of belief or trust. This capacity relieves the mind of a critical desire to reassess the grounds of settled judgment. Samuel Johnson observes that of an opinion that is no longer doubted, the evidences cease to be examined. When we believe in a product, we buy it with confidence. When we trust a person, we yield ourselves in fellowship.

Orderly conduct traces to a settled judgment. For example, a businessman gets off a commuter train and walks home. His conduct is orderly because his mind rests in the sufficiency of the evidences. He does not continually inquire: " Am I dreaming? Is sense perception reliable? Can I prove that I exist? " Hardly. He opens the door and greets his wife and family without demanding fresh proof that they *are* his wife and family. A wise man is critical about many things, but not all things. He does not believe contradictions, and he does not trust a fool. But he forthrightly believes whenever he confronts sufficient evidences. He is wise because he knows when to believe and when not to believe. He has faith.

1. *The Psychological Basis of Faith*

The capacity of belief or trust belongs to man as man. It is not necessarily a religious virtue. Suppose we are walking along a beach when suddenly we observe movement on the horizon. Another person is coming. We discover that this person is our friend Paul. A state of confidence is born. This state continues as long as the mind is satisfied with the sufficiency of the evidences. And by "mind" I do not mean bare rational assent. I mean the whole man in a responsible act of judgment.

Zealots often contend that faith requires a leap of the will or a risk of the intellect. Orthodoxy repudiates this in the name of both common sense and revelation. To believe on insufficient evidence — what is this but to believe what may not be true?

People make mistakes when they believe. They may even want something so badly that passion creates its own evidences. Reprehensible though these habits are, they nonetheless fall within the pale of man's general effort to conform the self to things as they are. But when a person *acknowledges* the deficiency of evidences and yet goes right on believing, he defends a position that is large with the elements of its own destruction. Any brand of inanity can be justified on such a principle.

Theologians speak a great deal about faith, but they do not always speak accurately. For example, Thomas Aquinas drew a sharp line between faith and knowledge. "Now, as was stated above, it is impossible that one and the same thing should be believed and seen by the same person. Hence it is equally impossible for one and the same thing to be an object of science and of belief for the same person."[1] This distinction overlooks the fact that *all* belief rests on authority. The authority can be direct or indirect. I may say, "I believe there is an ocean because I am standing in it" or "I believe the law of relativity because I have reviewed its mathematics." These illustrate *direct* authority — direct because the object, in each case, is immediately confronted. On another occasion I may say, "My doctor tells me I have a tumor" or "I see by this schedule that the train leaves at four." These illustrate *indirect* authority — indirect because a mediator stands between the object and my judgment. But this mediation in no way alters the axiom that all belief rests on authority. And what else *is* authority if not the power of sufficient evidences to elicit assent?

Protestant theologians frequently echo the Thomistic error. For example, Abraham Kuyper says, "By faith you are sure of all those things of which you have a *firm conviction,* but which conviction is *not* the outcome of observation or demonstration." [2] Kuyper forgets that the ground of belief is the *sufficiency,* not the kind or source, of evidence. Sometimes this sufficiency rises to demonstration — as in logic, mathematics, and geometry. In other cases it does not. A man of faith will not accept Euclid's propositions unless he confronts perfect demonstration. But he will accept the reality of pain on the testimony of a crushed finger.

Aristotle observed that an ability to decide what degree of precision may fairly be expected in any inquiry is the mark of an educated man. An educated man consults a physician, not a plumber, when he is ill; and when he consults a physician, he knows on what balance of evidence to believe. He expects sufficient evidence, but not mathematical demonstration.

2. *The Moral Quality in Faith*

Although faith traces to a satisfied judgment, a state of faith is not induced by the sheer display of sufficient evidences; for personal interest may build a protective wall around the intellect. Don Quixote is the literary symbol of this eventuality. When Sancho chided him for thinking that river mills were castles, Quixote was incensed at the effrontery of his squire. "Hold thy peace, Sancho," said Don Quixote; "though they look like mills they are not so; I have already told thee that enchantments transform things and change their proper shapes; I do not mean to say they really change them from one form to another, but that it seems as though they did, as experience proved in the transformation of Dulcinea, sole refuge of my hopes."

Every man has some sort of faith, for faith is the ground of orderly conduct. Even Quixote could distinguish between bread and sand at lunch time. Sancho often admired the sagacity of his master. Quixote's difficulty was that he failed to take this sagacity into the wider, and more critical, areas of life. He passed trivial tests, while failing the important.

As we move from formal truth (Two and two are four) to material truth (Is gambling wrong?), the threat of prejudice intensifies and the likelihood of dispassionate judgment abates. We often *see* what we *prefer* to see. Christian Science is an instructive example of this. A very precise objectivity goes into *The Christian Science Monitor*. The excellence of this paper is acclaimed by men of the fourth estate everywhere. But Christian Scientists cannot impartially judge evil, for they have surrendered their judgment to Mary Baker Eddy. When confronted with the most frightful cases of suffering, they reply, "Pain and death have no reality; they are errors of the material sense." It may be pleasant to believe that pain and death are errors of the material sense, but the cruel lines of reality are in no way changed by religious presuppositions.

Prejudice creeps in when we least suspect it. Samuel Johnson observed this with unusual candor. In his celebrated essay on Richard Savage he notes, " But this is only an instance of that partiality which almost every man indulges with regard to himself; the liberty of the press is a blessing when we are inclined to write against others, and a calamity when we find ourselves overborne by the multitude of our assailants; as the power of the crown is always thought too great by those who suffer by its influence, and too little by those in whose favor it is exerted; and a standing army is generally accounted necessary by those who command, and dangerous and oppressive by those who support it." No one can defeat the threat of prejudice unless he comes to himself and acknowledges the threat, and especially the manner in which the threat tinctures his own judgments. A man of faith is a man of character, and character implies a spiritual willingness to be honest before the facts. Pride says, " Believe what is congenial with personal interest." Honesty says, " Believe things as they are." Faithless men play fast and loose with evidences; their testimony is inadmissible. The rational life cannot get on with it unless the moral life is firm.

Jesus illustrated this by the native innocence of a child. " And calling to him a child, he put him in the midst of them, and said, ' Truly, I say to you, unless you turn and become like children, you will never enter the kingdom of heaven.' " (Matt. 18:2-3.) Prejudice does not corrupt the child's judgment; the true voice of reality is heard. The symbol of childhood is imperfect, of course, for the powers of prejudice are inchoate. But the symbol is useful, for we can become *like* a child. We can be honest in our approach to reality, and honest in conforming ourselves to it.

A child is a friend of common sense. He expects evidence, but not unreasonable evidence. He believes that the road to the park is uphill, but not uphill on the way back too. He believes in fairies, but not in *foolish* fairies. Even the preternatural world must conform to the limits of common sense.

Since a child stays in tune with life, he grasps things that often elude the wise of this world. (*a*) A child knows what truth is. Truth represents things as they are. If a child has taken cookies, but says he has not, he lies. And he knows it. His word does not conform to reality. (*b*) A child knows what goodness is. A good man is kind and thoughtful; a bad man is not. A child knows that love is the law of life, for he has experienced both the joys and the duty of love. (*c*) A child knows what beauty is. He can tell when his mother looks especially pretty. Excessive analysis does not corrupt his aesthetic intuitions. A cat is nice; so is a leaf.

Adults have more exacting standards than children; and between adults, according to the capacity of the mind, standards will differ. Boswell said that Johnson required more evidences because of his increased capacity. " He was only *willing* to believe; I *do* believe. The evidence is enough for me, though not for his great mind. What will not fill a quart bottle will fill a pint bottle."

But this observation in no way depresses the force of Christ's counsel that we must become like little children. Great minds and little children have important things in common. They are friends of general wisdom; they proportion their expectations to the nature of reality before them; they stay with the true order of things.

Culture is purest when the tribe interacts with reality in a free and natural manner. The wisdom of folklore is timeless because childlike values are raised to philosophic status. The common man distrusts sophistication; he is a friend of the straightforward.

The opposite of childlike trust is hardness of heart. While Quixote was *blinded,* hardness of heart is *perverse*. This is proved by the manner in which refractory evidences are resisted. And there is no more graphic illustration of this than the crucifixion of Jesus Christ.

Whereas the common man came to Jesus gladly, the hardened heart took up stones to stone him. " It is to fulfill the word that is written in their law, ' They hated me without a cause.' " (John 15:25.) To hate without a cause means to hate without a *justifiable* cause. Resentment is a desperate expedient. It seeks to nullify distasteful evidences. Carlyle wisely observes that there are some attitudes like jealousy, which, though causeless, yet cannot be removed by reasons as apparent as demonstration can make any truth.

Hardness of heart invalidates common sense. Pharaoh illustrates this pathos. Though given abundant proof that the Lord was God, he was so opinionated that no amount of evidence could unlearn him. In the end Pharaoh destroyed himself. Any child could have told him he was playing the fool.

Prejudice curtailed the effectiveness of Jesus' ministry. " And he did not do many mighty works there, because of their unbelief." (Matt. 13:58.) Jesus was *able* to do many mighty works, but a display of Messianic credentials before resentment would have been pointless pedagogy. *All* learning is based on humility before the facts.

3. *The Two Kinds of Faith*

Faith is the capacity of belief or trust. This capacity is expressed in two separate, though mutually supporting, ways. *To believe a thing* is general faith; *to trust a person* is vital faith. Let us examine these in this order.

General faith is a resting of the mind in the sufficiency of the evidences. Two rules govern general faith: *first,* withhold judgment until the evidences are sufficient; *secondly,* act consistently on all warranted belief. A life of faith is a life of wisdom. Foolishness either believes when it should doubt (the cultic mind), or it doubts when it should believe (hardness of heart). The cultic mind courts credulity; hardness of heart courts incredulity. Credulity believes too soon; incredulity, not soon enough.

Orthodoxy has little patience with the cliché that religious people have faith while men of science and philosophy have knowledge. General faith spans the entire human enterprise. To believe on insufficient evidence is folly, not faith. Faith may stress *commitment,* whereas knowledge stresses *apprehension,* but both make an equal draft on facts " out there." Whether we believe the word of man or the Word of God, we believe because we are satisfied with the sufficiency of the evidences. And we deem the evidences to be no less objective in the one case than we do in the other.

Vital faith is richer than general faith because the act of trusting a person calls for a greater measure of commitment than the act of believing a thing. The meaning of geometry can be understood by the intellect alone, but the meaning of a person remains veiled until the intellect is joined by the intuitions of the heart. If we seek access to another person, we must come by way of revelation — the revelation that he makes when we show spontaneous signs of receiving the dignity of his life. In other words, we must proportion our methods of knowing to the kind of reality under consideration. Philosophy is thought; pudding is tasted; and a person is encountered in fellowship.

Whenever genuine fellowship is enjoyed, the distinction between faith and knowledge disappears, for to *know* another person is to *trust* him. " Now Adam knew Eve his wife, and she conceived and bore Cain." (Gen. 4:1.) The marital due requires such a total act of personal surrender that it is equated with knowledge. Again, " I never knew you," says the Lord; " depart from me, you evildoers." (Matt. 7:23.) While the Lord *apprehends* evildoers, he does not know them in the only way that counts, namely, fellowship. Sin issues in autonomy, not surrender.

Vital faith is not unique to the religious life, let alone to Christianity. Like general faith, it belongs to the order of man as man. When a little boy sees his friend with a sack of candy he says, " *You know me!* " And he certainly does not mean that his friend can give an intellectual account of his person. He means, " We are on speaking terms; we like each other; so, share your jelly beans! " He appeals to the moral obligation in fellowship — the obligation to surrender benefits as well as the self.

General faith is the foundation of vital faith. This is true on every level of life. Before a husband can embrace his wife, he must be convinced that it is his wife, and not a stranger, before him. The same is true in our approach to God. We must be convinced that we are confronting *God,* not a counterfeit.

General faith is a resting of the mind in the sufficiency of the evidences; vital faith is cordial trust. General faith is only censured when it pretends to do the work of vital faith. For example, the demons are credited with general faith. They address Jesus Christ with language that is strikingly similar to that used by the angels. "You believe that God is one; you do well. Even the demons believe — and shudder." (James 2:19.) The faith of demons profits nothing because it is general faith and nothing more. It is not "a vital faith, such as is required in the gospel; a living and active principle, serving at once to connect us with Christ, and to constrain us to live no longer to ourselves, but to him that died for us, and that rose again. In a word, it must be 'the faith which worketh by love.' LOVE is the sum of God's law, and the spring of all acceptable obedience." [3]

The difference between general and vital faith ought to be clear by now. When a person assents to truth, or when he believes in an object, he commits *part* of himself. This is general faith. But when he trusts another person, he commits the *whole* of himself. This is vital faith. Fellowship is a union of life with life. The essence of one person passes into that of another.

4. *The Trial of Faith*

Faith is often put to trial. For example, Cinderella believed in the ultimate triumph of goodness. She rested in the sufficiency of the evidences. But when her wicked stepmother gained the upper hand and Cinderella could not go to the ball, faith was on trial. Cinderella ran to the garden and wept. But to the relief of children — and all who are children in heart — a fairy godmother appeared and renewed the evidences. Faith revived.

A Christian believes that God is sovereign over the affairs of men. Yet the Christian lives in a "world with devils filled." The righteous suffer and the unrighteous prosper. The heroes of the faith "were stoned, they were sawn in two, they were killed with the sword; they went about in skins of sheep and goats, destitute, afflicted, ill-treated " (Heb. 11:37). The heroes of the faith passed the trial of faith. The present evil world prompted them to look for a better world — a world with foundations, whose builder and maker is God.

The trial of faith does not mean that a Christian rallies courage to act on insufficient evidence. To say it is Saturday, when it is Sunday; or that one possesses gold, when he is sifting sand; or that the stomach is sated, when one is starving — these are signs of foolishness, not faith. Faith is the subjective element in *warranted* belief; and warranted belief rests in the sufficiency of the evidences.

A Christian is like a physicist at a magic show. Each successful trick is a threat to the physicist's faith in the law of uniformity. Large rabbits are drawn from small hats, and a lady floats through the air. The physicist is admittedly baffled. But his faith is not overturned, for the law of uniformity is settled on scientific, not private, grounds. In a similar way, a Christian keeps the promises of God before him. " The true way to have faith strengthened is not to consider the difficulties in the way of the thing promised, but the character and resources of God, who has made the promise." [4] Conflicting evidences may *baffle* the Christian, but they do not cast him down; for the promises of God are decided on Biblical, not empirical, grounds.

Christians often pray, " I believe; help my unbelief! " (Mark 9:24). And they pray thus because they are suspended between voluntary belief and involuntary unbelief. Ambivalence of this sort is *normal* to Christian faith. " When we inculcate, that faith ought to be certain and secure, we conceive not of a certainty attended with no doubt, or of a security interrupted by no anxiety; but we rather affirm, that believers have a perpetual conflict with their own diffidence, and are far from placing their consciences in a placid calm, never disturbed by any storms. Yet, on the other hand, we deny, however they may be afflicted, that they ever fall and depart from that certain confidence which they have conceived in the divine mercy." [5]

The difference between voluntary belief and involuntary unbelief can easily be illustrated. Suppose we reach our favorite picnic spot, only to worry whether we locked the front door. To settle our minds, we think back on the events of the morning. We decide that the door is, in fact, locked. But this deliberation does not eradicate the threat of involuntary unbelief. Anxiety may linger on the edge of our dominant affections. About all we can do is see that anxiety does not ruin our picnic. " The door *is* locked! " we remind ourselves. And having labeled the source of our problem, we let the matter go.

Deliverance from involuntary unbelief will not be enjoyed until we walk by sight in the Kingdom of Heaven. When we receive our resurrection bodies, the discord in our hearts will end. But until then, the Christian must deliberately superintend his own affections. " Keep your heart with all vigilance; for from it flow the springs of life." (Prov. 4:23.)

Since it is easier for God not to be God than to fail in his covenantal promises, involuntary unbelief is never a decisive threat to the Christian.

> " Though the fig tree do not blossom,
> nor fruit be on the vines,
> the produce of the olive fail
> and the fields yield no food,
> the flock be cut off from the fold
> and there be no herd in the stalls,
> yet I will rejoice in the Lord,
> I will joy in the God of my salvation."
> (Hab. 3:17-18.)

Collateral Reading

1. The theology of faith: Calvin, *Institutes,* III. ii.
2. The psychology of faith: Warfield, B. B., " On Faith in Its Psychological Aspects," in *Biblical and Theological Studies,* pp. 375-403. The Presbyterian and Reformed Publishing Company, 1952.

III.

Authority

As we turn to the ground of authority in orthodoxy, it should be observed that we are *not* examining the order in which a sinner comes to Christ. The order is that of apologetics, not evangelism. "Always be prepared to make a defense to any one who calls you to account for the hope that is in you." (I Peter 3:15.)

1. The Living and Written Word of God

We have defined orthodoxy as "that branch of Christendom which limits the ground of religious authority to the Bible." The important element in this definition is the term "limits." All branches of Christendom, whatever their stripe, salute the Bible as a general source of religious information. Apart from Scripture we would have no access to the redemptive events. Orthodoxy is unique in that it argues for the *plenary* inspiration of Scripture. The Bible, and the Bible alone, is the Word of God written.

Unless the claims of orthodoxy are spelled out with care, however, they may connote an odious Biblicism. For example, critics sometimes say, "We believe the Bible on the authority of Jesus Christ, and not the other way around." This is supposed to be a more precise way of stating things. But orthodoxy has *always* insisted that the written Word does not commend itself unless the heart is confronted by the living Word. Paul did not see Christ in Scripture until he met Christ on the Damascus road. The Bible is the Word of God "out there," whether or not anyone is confronted by it; but it does not address the heart as the Word of God until Christ is met in personal fellowship. The living Word is the soul of the written Word.

Let us illustrate this. Suppose Robert receives a letter from his beloved, Wilma. The letter is more than ink and paper; it is a vehicle of Wilma's soul. But only Robert can perceive this. Outsiders may read the letter, but only love can divine the affairs of love. Similarly, outsiders may read the Bible. But they cannot perceive the soul of Christ, for they are not in fellowship with Christ. Fellowship knows *Christ,* not *about* Christ. This is knowledge by acquaintance.

But Wilma's letter is more than a medium of confrontation; it is also a propositional revelation of her will. Wilma sends her love, but she also asks Robert to meet her at the railroad station. Her words *command* as well as charm; they *communicate* as well as affect. Were Robert to rush to the airport, rather than to the railroad station, he would fail as a lover.

This principle is no less true of Scripture. The Word of God commands as well as charms; it communicates as well as affects. " If you love me," says Jesus Christ, " you will keep my commandments." (John 14:15.) To say we are confronted by Christ, when we do not obey him — what is this but to offend the work of love? Love is fettered by the will of the beloved. " He who does not love me does not keep my words." (V. 24.)

Therefore, in the one act of reading Scripture, we meet Christ in two complementary ways. *First,* we confront Christ's person. " By this we know that we abide in him and he in us, because he has given us of his own Spirit." (I John 4:13.) *Secondly,* we receive a propositional revelation of Christ's will. " In many and various ways God spoke of old to our fathers by the prophets; but in these last days he has spoken to us by a Son." (Heb. 1:1-2.) These two elements cannot be separated without offending the unity of revelation.

The written Word is the locus of confrontation with the living Word. If we extend this locus, we have no criterion by which to test for error. And when the church cannot test for error, it cannot claim truth; for its claim may be one expression of an error for which there is no test. The church's sole message is the gospel, and the gospel is the substance of the written Word. God made a covenant with Abraham, and Jesus Christ is the blessing of this covenant. Everything in Scripture either looks forward to Christ or flows from him. " Do not think that I shall accuse you to the Father; it is Moses who accuses you, on whom you set your hope. If you believed Moses, you would believe me, for he wrote of me. But if you do not believe his writings, how will you believe my words? " (John 5:45-46.)

2. *Jesus Christ and the Old Testament*

When orthodoxy is asked why it accepts the Old Testament as the inspired Word of God, it answers, Because Jesus Christ, the Lord of the church, did. The orthodox apologist rests his case on this single datum. " For him who has been brought to the Christ, and who on his knees worships him as his Lord and his God, the end of all contradiction is hereby reached. When the Christ, whose Spirit witnessed beforehand in the prophets, attributes such authority to the Scripture of the Old Covenant, and by his apostles indicates the ground for that authority in the theopneusty, there is no power that can prevent the recognition of that authority by him who believes in Jesus. Not to recognize it would avenge itself in the representation that in the very holiest things Christ had wholly mistaken himself. This would imply *the loss of his Savior*." [1]

Jesus entered a society that was already bound by a canon of sacred writings. Malachi was the last of the written prophets. An interval of some four hundred years separated Malachi from the birth of Christ. Jerusalem was restored; the Maccabees performed their heroic deeds; the Temple was rebuilt by Herod; and Israel was overtaken first by Greece, then by Rome. When Jesus began his public ministry, he in no way contradicted the prevailing Jewish attitude toward the authority of the Law and the Prophets. On the contrary, he appealed to this corpus of revelation when validating his own Messianic claims. " We observe that our Lord, throughout the entire duration of his ministry, represents himself as fulfilling, in person, the scheme of the former covenant; we know, too, that he has made the Old Testament the basis of his teaching; continually employing it, as it was received in his time by the Jews, without letting fall the slightest hint that any portion of it was done away. So far from stating anything to this effect, he has expressed himself in a manner which proves the very reverse; making use of language by which he has not only defined the permanent authority of the Old Testament, but also indicated its true place in the new dispensation." [2]

Certainly the Jews would never have defended and preserved a canon of documents that condemned their own practices, and that placed them under oppressive judicial burdens, unless they believed they were in possession of divine oracles. Jesus shared this conviction.

Even radical critics acknowledge that Jesus believed in the divine authority of the Old Testament. Such critics merely reject the Lordship of Christ. Orthodoxy does not. *When Christ speaks of the Scriptures, he means the Old Testament; and when he says that the Scriptures cannot be broken, he means they have the force of law and are to be received in the church on divine authority.*

3. *Jesus Christ and the Details of the Old Testament*

Jesus assigned authority to the details, as well as to the whole, of the Old Testament. " In Matt. xxii.44, the strength of Jesus' argument hangs on the single word *Lord*. ' The Lord said *unto my Lord* '; yea, even more precisely, on the single *iod*. The emphasis falls on the ' *my* Lord.' In John x.35 the entire argument falls to the ground, except the one word ' gods ' have absolute authority. In the same way it can be shown, in a number of Jesus' arguments from the Scripture, that in the main they do not rest upon the general contents, but often upon a single word or a single letter. The theory therefore of a general *tendency* in the spiritual domain, which in the Old Testament should merely have an *advisory* authority, finds no support in Jesus." [3]

Since Jesus rested his Messianic office on the authority of the Old Testament, a Christian offends consistent procedure if he accepts Christ's Messianic office, but rejects the divine authority of the Old Testament. In John, ch. 10, for example: " Jesus' defense takes the form of an appeal to Scripture; and it is important to observe how he makes this appeal. In the first place, he adduces the Scriptures as law: 'Is it not written in your law?' he demands. The passage of Scripture which he adduces is not written in that portion of Scripture which was more specifically called 'the law,' that is to say, the Pentateuch; nor in any portion of Scripture of formally legal contents. It is written in the Book of Psalms; and in a particular psalm which is as far as possible from presenting the external characteristics of legal enactment (Ps. lxxxii.6). When Jesus adduces this passage, then, as written in the 'law' of the Jews, he does it, not because it stands in this psalm, but because it is a part of Scripture at large. In other words, he here ascribes legal authority to the entirety of Scripture, in accordance with a conception common enough among the Jews (cf. Jn. xii.34). . . . But our Lord, determined to drive his appeal to Scripture home, sharpens the point to the utmost by adding with the highest emphasis: 'and the Scripture cannot be broken.' This is the reason why it is worth-while to appeal to what is 'written in the law,' because 'the Scripture cannot be broken.' . . . It is impossible for the Scripture to be annulled, its authority to be withstood, or denied. The movement of thought is to the effect that, because it is impossible for the Scripture . . . to be withstood, therefore this particular Scripture which is cited must be taken as of irrefragable authority. What we have here is, therefore, the strongest possible assertion of the indefectible authority of Scripture." [4]

4. *The Witness of Christ's Enemies*

If further evidence were needed to establish the authority of the Old Testament, it would come from those who were resentful of Christ and who missed no opportunity to accuse him. Since Christ's enemies scrutinized everything he did and said, their word is strong collateral proof of what Jesus really taught. " For three years Jesus had been most narrowly watched by the Sanhedrin, and every word he spoke had been carefully sifted. At that time there were two holy things in Israel: their Scripture and their Temple. Of these two Jesus gave up the Temple, of which he said that not one stone would be left upon the other; while, on the contrary, of the Scripture he declared, that no jot or tittle of it shall pass till all shall be fulfilled. Concerning his speech against the Temple, complaint was made against him, though the form of the charge was unjust. If he had uttered a single word against the Scripture of the Old Testament, he would certainly have been similarly accused. With reference to this, however, you observe no charge, not even a weak reproach, and from this it may be inferred, that in this matter of the Scriptures his enemies had no fault to find with him." [5] When Jesus said he was the Messiah of the Old Testament, the Jews rejected his claim. But they did not reject his assertion that the Old Testament was the Word of God.

5. *The Accommodation of Christ to His Culture*

Critics often say that when Christ defended the Old Testament, he was simply accommodating himself to prevailing religious opinion. But such a hypothesis offends the most patent evidence in the Gospels. Whenever religious tradition was inharmonious with the claims of the Old Testament, Christ defended the Old Testament. Take the instance of the murder of Zacharias, in Matt., ch. 23. " To say that Christ accommodates himself to the popular view without adopting it himself, contradicts the connection of thought. Christ is denouncing [*sic*] the judgment of God upon the Pharisees. This would be an idle threat if there were no such series of martyrs, and no true account of them in the Old Testament scriptures." [6] And what is true in this one incident is true of all other incidents in Christ's public ministry. " Christ neither denies the existence of spirits in order to conciliate the Sadducees; nor does he instruct the woman of Samaria in doctrines which he opposed before the Jews. . . . In a word, we find Christ quoting Moses and the prophets to friend and to foe; to Pharisee and to Sadducee; to the people and to his disciples; in the desert and in the Temple; at the commencement of his ministry and at its close; in exposition by acts, and exposition by doctrine — combining, on all occasions, the Old Testament with the new revelation as being conveyed by the same Spirit." [7]

After his resurrection, when his human nature was on the threshold of final glory, Jesus maintained the same attitude toward the authority of Scripture. " And beginning with Moses and all the prophets, he interpreted to them in all the scriptures the things concerning himself." (Luke 24:27.) " If such reports of Jesus' ideas about the Scripture were very rare, if they appeared for their own purposes only, or if it was their aim to formulate a certain theory of inspiration, then . . . they would not possess such a historic value to us; but since there is no trace of such a design and no insertion of a system is thought of, and only the use is shown which Jesus made of the Scripture amid the most varied circumstances and with all sorts of applications, from these reports it is historically certain, for him also who does not reckon with inspiration, that Jesus judged the Scriptures thus, and not otherwise." [8]

The danger with this construction, of course, is that zealots may press it to an unwarranted extreme. Purely literary questions *cannot* be settled by an appeal to Christ's testimony. Whether The Book of Judges was composed by one inspired author, or whether it is the work of several redactors, is a question of criticism, not Christology.

6. *The Union of Christ and the Father*

Some say that Jesus was *mistaken* in his view of Scripture. The assumption is that if Jesus had enjoyed the benefits of modern criticism, he would have entertained a different attitude toward the Old Testament. Orthodoxy rejects this because it destroys our faith in God the Father. Let us establish this by setting down a series of propositions.

Proposition One: Jesus is Emmanuel, " God with us." When the eternal Son became incarnate, he did not forfeit his divine attributes. Continuing what he was, he took on what he was not. Jesus merely emptied himself of the right to express unveiled deity. This was the true kenosis. The Son subordinated himself to the will of the Father for the sake of redeeming the world.

Proposition Two: All that Jesus did or said transpired in the human nature. It is an unfortunate formula, one quite foreign to Scripture, that Jesus " hungered in his human nature " but " performed miracles in his divine nature." The *entire Messianic office* was confined to the divine person in human nature. Jesus was the last Adam; he was the federal head of a new and holy race.

Proposition Three: The human nature of Jesus was so perfectly united with the divine person, and the divine person was so perfectly united with the will of the Father, that all that Jesus did or said derived from the Father. "Jesus said to them, 'Truly, truly, I say to you, the Son can do nothing of his own accord, but only what he sees the Father doing; for whatever he does, that the Son does likewise.'" (John 5:19.) "I can do nothing on my own authority; as I hear, I judge; and my judgment is just, because I seek not my own will but the will of him who sent me." (V. 30.)

Since Christ was so intimately united with the Father, we cannot impugn the judgment of Christ without impugning the judgment of the Father. Jesus and the Father were one in teaching as well as essence. "For I have not spoken on my own authority; the Father who sent me has himself given me commandment what to say and what to speak." (Ch. 12:49.) "Do you not believe that I am in the Father and the Father in me? The words that I say to you I do not speak on my own authority; but the Father who dwells in me does his works." (Ch. 14:10.) "The word which you hear is not mine but the Father's who sent me." (V. 24.)

There is only one consistent position for the church. *Since Jesus received his doctrine from the Father, everything that Jesus says is true on divine authority.* Any other position leads to skepticism. "Can he have been — mistaken, mistaken — with respect to holiest things, in what must be to us the ground and source of our faith! Mistaken also, therefore, in assigning, on the basis of the Scripture, a high Messianic character to himself! But the very idea is incompatible with the confession of Jesus' divine nature. Erring in what is holy is no mere failure in intellect, but betrays a state of ruin of one's whole inner being. In the sinner, therefore, a mistake is natural, but not in one who is holy. . . . The conflict, which is begun in order to rob us of the Scripture as Holy Scripture, can have no other tendency than to rob us of the Christ. If the Holy Scripture . . . falls, then Jesus was a man and nothing more, who was mistaken in the centrum of what was holy, and who consequently can neither escape from the fellowship of sin, nor yet in what is holiest and tenderest be your absolute guide." [9]

7. The View of the Apostles

Christ appointed an apostolate to bear witness to all that he did and said. Even as Christ was sent to declare the will of the Father, so the apostles were sent to declare the will of Christ.

Whoever reads the New Testament with an eye to fairness will perceive that the apostles defended the same view of Scripture that Jesus did. Scripture has the force of law; the Word of God cannot be broken. "This appears clearly in Acts ii.24, 25, where Peter says, 'It was not possible that he should be holden of death.' And why does he deem this impossible? Because Jesus was the Son of God? Undoubtedly for this also; of this, however, Peter makes no mention, but states as the only reason that it was thus written in Ps. xvi.: 'Neither wilt thou give thy Holy One to see corruption.' Hence the 'impossibility' rests upon the fact that the opposite to this was written in the Old Testament; an argument which suits only with the supposition that the Old Testament furnishes us with the program of what *must* happen according to God's counsel and will." [10]

"All scripture," says Paul, "is inspired by God and profitable for teaching, for reproof, for correction, and for training in righteousness, that the man of God may be complete, equipped for every good work." (II Tim. 3:16-17.) "It is manifestly impossible, however we translate the words, that St. Paul could have meant by them anything else than the whole body of the Old Testament writings: since no Jew — and he was addressing a man of Jewish descent, to whose intimate acquaintance with the sacred literature of the nation he had just appealed — could have attached any other meaning to his language; or could have supposed that, in the expressions here employed, some particular writings only, or certain portions of them, were referred to as the work of the Spirit of God." [11]

Although Peter heard the Voice of God on the Mount of Transfiguration, he assigns a more sure foundation to the written Scriptures than to the Voice itself. "And we have the prophetic word made more sure. You will do well to pay attention to this as to a lamp shining in a dark place, until the day dawns and the morning star rises in your hearts." (II Peter 1:19.)

To trace this sort of evidence through the entire apostolic testimony would be to dwell on the obvious. " The uniform manner of speaking of the Old Testament which we trace in the sayings and writings of Christ and his apostles in the New — is such as to be wholly incompatible with any other idea than that of its full and verbal inspiration: and cannot but convey to a simple reader the impression that they regarded every word of that Testament as divine." [12]

Since the apostles were commissioned to define Christian doctrine, the evidence for the authority of Scripture is precisely as strong as that for any other doctrine in the Christian faith. " It is the same weight and amount of evidence precisely which is adducible for the truth of the doctrines of the incarnation, of the Trinity, of the divinity of Christ, of justification by faith, of regeneration by the Holy Spirit, of the resurrection of the body, of life everlasting. . . . The question is not *how* they [the apostles] teach a doctrine, but *do* they teach it; and when that question is once settled affirmatively, the weight of evidence that commends this doctrine to us as true is the same in every case; and that is the whole body of evidence which goes to show that the Biblical writers are trustworthy as teachers of doctrine. The Biblical doctrine of inspiration, therefore, has in its favor just this whole weight and amount of evidence. It follows on the one hand that it cannot rationally be rejected save on the ground of evidence which will outweigh the whole body of evidence which goes to authenticate the Biblical writers as trustworthy witnesses to and teachers of doctrine. And it follows, on the other hand, that if the Biblical doctrine of inspiration is rejected, our freedom from its trammels is bought logically at the somewhat serious cost of discrediting the evidence which goes to show that the Biblical writers are trustworthy as teachers of doctrine. In this sense, the fortunes of distinctive Christianity are bound up with those of the Biblical doctrine of inspiration." [13]

This argument is so decisive that it bears restating in other language. " We do not adopt the doctrine of the plenary inspiration of

Scripture on sentimental grounds, nor even, as we have already had occasion to remark on a priori or general grounds of whatever kind. We adopt it specifically because it is taught us as truth by Christ and his apostles, in the Scriptural record of their teaching, and the evidence for its truth is, therefore, as we have also already pointed out, precisely that evidence, in weight and amount, which vindicates for us the trustworthiness of Christ and his apostles as teachers of doctrine." [14]

8. *The Canon of the Old Testament*

Authenticity is ordinarily distinct from credibility. It might be proved, for example, that a copy of Lewis Carroll's *Alice's Adventures in Wonderland* is authentic. But this would not make the book credible. In the case of the Biblical canon, however, authenticity ensures credibility; for canonicity respects the *extent,* not the *fact,* of an inspired text.

The question of the canon is settled by historical evidences, not by personal confrontation with Christ. " The teaching of the Holy Ghost, while indispensable to a saving apprehension of Biblical truth, is not available at this point. The Holy Spirit teaches in regard to the credibility, but not in regard to the canonicity of Scripture." [15]

Orthodoxy settles the authenticity of the Old Testament in the only way that it can or should be settled, namely, by an appeal to Christ and the apostles. " The question of the canon of the Old Testament being by the principles clearly deducible from the statements of Christ and his apostles limited to this, what were the books which composed the received Jewish canon at that time? There is no material difficulty in determining that point. We have sufficient materials for ascertaining what books were then generally received by the Jews as canonical. We have these materials to a large extent in the New Testament itself, in the testimony of the contemporary Jewish authors, Josephus and Philo; in the universal and unwavering belief of the Jews from that period to the present day; and in the testimonies of some of the early Christian fathers, particularly that of Melito (preserved by Eusebius), who lived in the second century, and who made the investigating of the canon of the Old Testament an object of peculiar attention and of diligent inquiry. The books which compose the Protestant canon of the Old Testament alone were received as of divine authority by the Jews of our Savior's days, and therefore these alone received his sanction." [16] Christ and the apostles accepted the prevailing threefold division of the Jewish canon: the Law, the Prophets, and the Writings. This decided the matter for the early church, and it decides it for orthodoxy in any age.

9. *The Canon of the New Testament*

Although the New Testament canon is established in the same manner as that of the Old Testament, the steps in the argument are a bit more involved. Let us establish this by a series of propositions.

Proposition One: Christ defended the divine authority of the Old Testament canon. And he received this judgment from the Father.

Proposition Two: Christ did *not* invest the Old Testament with authority. The Old Testament anteceded his Messianic office. A process of revelation was already at work in history.

Proposition Three: The Old Testament, on divine authority, bears witness to its own incompleteness; it looks to a revelation yet to come. Thus, the " same *necessity of the Scripture,* which existed for the manifestation of the prophetic dispensation, was here repeated." [17]

Proposition Four: The apostles were commissioned to take the gospel to all nations, and there was only one way in which this could be done. That was by the medium of inspired documents. Hence, the apostles address the church with the authority of *prophets.* The New Testament writers " do not for an instant imagine themselves, as ministers of a new covenant, less in possession of the Spirit of God than the ministers of the old covenant: they freely recognize, indeed, that they have no sufficiency of themselves, but they know that God has made them sufficient (2 Cor. iii.5.6). They prosecute their work of proclaiming the gospel, therefore, in full confidence that they speak 'by the Holy Spirit' (1 Pet. i.12), to whom they attribute both the matter and form of their teaching (1 Cor. ii.13). They, therefore, speak with the utmost assurance of their teaching (Gal. i.7.8); and they issue commands with the completest authority (1 Thess. iv.2.14; 2 Thess. iii.6.12), making it, indeed, the test of whether one has the Spirit that he should recognize what they demand as commandments of God (1 Cor. xiv.37)." [18] " I adjure you by the Lord that this letter be read to all the brethren." (I Thess. 5:27.)

Proposition Five: The canon of the New Testament was decided by the apostles themselves, for they alone knew what documents were inspired, and thus were normative for the church. " All doubt is dispelled when we observe the New Testament writers placing the writings of one another in the same category of ' Scripture ' with the books of the Old Testament. The same Paul who, in 2 Tim. iii.16, declared that ' every ' or ' all scripture is God-breathed ' had already written in 1 Tim. v.18: ' For the scripture saith, Thou shalt not muzzle the ox when he treadeth out the corn. And, The laborer is worthy of his hire.' The first clause here is derived from Deuteronomy and the second from the Gospel of Luke, though both are cited as together constituting, or better, forming part of the ' Scripture ' which Paul adduces as so authoritative as by its mere citation to end all strife. . . . And the same Peter who declared that every ' prophecy of scripture ' was the product of men who spoke ' from God,' being ' borne ' by the Holy Ghost (2 Pet. i.21), in this same epistle (iii.16), places Paul's Epistles in the category of Scripture along with whatever other books deserve that name. For Paul, says he, wrote these epistles, not out of his own wisdom, but ' according to the wisdom given to him,' and though there are some things in them hard to be understood, yet it is only ' the ignorant and unstedfast ' who wrest these difficult passages — as what else could be expected of men who wrest ' also the other Scriptures ' (obviously the Old Testament is meant) — ' unto their own destruction '? " [19]

The church merely had to determine whether a particular book bore the marks of apostolic authority. This judgment involved a sifting of historical evidences. The debate was over authenticity, not credibility. And the doubts about authenticity were not resolved until at least the fourth century. " The point to which the doubts that were entertained attached was this, and this only, *whether or not these books were really written by the men whose names they bore, and to whom they were generally ascribed*. Now, considering the condition of the world and the state of the churches, the means of intercourse, etc., there is no difficulty whatever in conceiving that writings published in one part of the world might be long in becoming known in another, and that even after they were in some measure known, it might not be very easy for some time to ascertain precisely their history, and to procure satisfactory evidence as to the matters of fact alleged concerning them. . . . There were many apocryphal books in circulation pretending to be written by apostles, and the churches were on their guard against being deceived by any false pretenses on this subject. Paul encouraged the churches to jealousy upon this point, by virtually telling them . . . that they were to receive no epistles of his as genuine unless the salutation was written with his own hand. And this salutary caution and jealousy they seem to have faithfully practiced — a fact which at once accounts for the doubts entertained for a time in some quarters of the church, about some books in regard to which they had not for the present access to any satisfactory evidence that they were the productions of apostles or inspired men, and gives great weight to their testimony in favor of those in regard to which no doubt was ever entertained, and also to the ultimate testimony of the church in general in favor of the others likewise, after the doubts which had once attached to them had been removed, i.e., after satisfactory and conclusive evidence had been diffused over the whole extent of the Christian church that they were the production of the men whose names they bore, and to whom they were generally ascribed." [20]

Let us linger with this question a bit longer, for the issue is very critical. The church did *not* invest the canon with authority; nor was the gift of inspiration required to decide which books bore apostolic marks and which did not. "*The evidence by which the canonical authority of the books of the New Testament is proved, is the same in kind as that by which we establish their genuineness. The books are proved to be genuine when it is shown that they were the productions of the men whose names they bear*. . . . Now there really never was any such thing as what seems to be conceived of under the designation of establishing or settling the canon of the New Testament. The canonical authority of the books, their right to be regarded as an authoritative communication of the will of God, depends entirely upon the actual matter of fact of their having been composed by divinely inspired authors; and the settlement of the canon properly means nothing else than the establishment of this as a matter of fact by the appropriate evidence with respect to those books on whose behalf a claim to canonical authority has been put forth. . . . The question as to when the books which compose the canon of the New Testament were first collected into one volume is a mere matter of historical curiosity, and has really nothing to do with settling their canonical authority, though these two questions have been commonly confounded by those who have labored to involve this whole matter in obscurity and uncertainty. Their canonical authority depends upon their authorship, and we estimate the testimonies, whether of individuals or churches or councils, the whole mass of quotations, references, and other materials derived from the works of ancient writers, *upon the ordinary recognized principles applicable to the historical evidence of a matter of fact.*" [21] We submit to the judgment of the early church because we have no reason to question the ground on which the sufficiency of evidences was established. If God ordained the church to *hear* the Word of the Son, the means to this end were also ordained.

10. *The Problem of Mark and Luke*

But if only *apostles* were authorized to give a normative interpretation of Christ's life, death, and resurrection, why are Mark and Luke in the canon? The answer is, Mark and Luke belonged to the " circle of revelation." The apostles validated the work of Mark and Luke; and it is apostolic *validation,* not apostolic *authorship,* which entitles a book to a place in the canon. " That the apostles so imposed the Old Testament on the churches which they founded . . . can be denied by none. And in imposing new books on the same churches, by the same apostolical authority, they did not confine themselves to books of their own composition. It is the Gospel According to Luke, a man who was not an apostle, which Paul parallels in 1 Tim. v.18 with Deuteronomy as equally 'Scripture' with it, in the first extant quotation of a New Testament book as Scripture." [22] Mark and Luke are inspired; they served as an extension of the apostolic college. "Mark wrote his Gospel under the immediate direction and guidance of the apostle Peter, who in the end of his first epistle described him as Marcus, his son, and intimated that he was then with him in Babylon; and . . . Luke wrote his Gospel and The Acts under the immediate guidance and direction of Paul, whom he accompanied on his voyage to Rome, and with whom he remained for some time in that city." [23] The church enrolled Mark and Luke in the canon for precisely the same reason that it did the writings of Paul: namely, because they bore marks of authenticity.

Some may wonder why the New Testament does not list its own books, thus settling the question of the canon by divine inspiration. But a list of books would by no means resolve the problem of authenticity. The church would have to assure itself that the documents in hand correspond with those in the canonical list. This would again cast the church on a quest for historical evidences.

The search for authenticity will never end. The early church settled the canon, for it had access to the relevant evidences. But the modern church must continue to sift and classify the variant readings in the present documents. The original manuscripts are all lost.

11. *Conclusion*

Since orthodoxy defends the plenary inspiration of Scripture, it is always tempted to make propositional revelation an end in itself. Whenever it yields to this temptation, it offends its own presuppositions. Propositional revelation is an instrumental value; it is designed to bring us into fellowship with Jesus Christ. "These are written that you may believe that Jesus is the Christ, the Son of God, and that believing you may have life in his name." (John 20:31.) "Inspiration is no isolated fact, which stands by itself. He who takes it in this sense arrives at some sort of Koran, but not at the Holy Scripture. In that case the principium of knowing (*cognoscendi*) is taken entirely apart from the principium of being (*essendi*), and causes the appearance of an exclusively intellectual product which is outside of reality. We then would have an inspiration which dictated intellectually, and could not communicate to us anything but a doctrine and a law." [24]

The gospel is the good news that God entered history and did something that man could not do for himself. The redemptive events are the foundation of the normative interpretation, and not the other way around. To conceive of the Bible as the primary revelation is heresy. If there had been no redemptive events, there would be no theology.

COLLATERAL READING

1. The definitive expression of the orthodox apologetic: Warfield, B. B., "The Real Problem of Inspiration," in *The Inspiration and Authority of the Bible*, pp. 169–226. The Presbyterian and Reformed Publishing Company, 1948.

2. Handy reviews of the orthodox apologetic: Candlish, Robert S., *Reason and Revelation*, pp. 9–90, T. Nelson & Sons, London, 1859; M'Intyre, David M., *The Divine Authority of the Scriptures of the Old Testament*, S. W. Partridge & Co., London, n.d.; and Patton, Francis L., *The Inspiration of the Scriptures*, Presbyterian Board of Publication & Sabbath-school Work, 1922. A prolix review: Burgon, John William, *Inspiration and Interpretation*, Marshall Brothers, London, 1905. A catechetical review: Hodge, A. A., *Outlines of Theology*, pp. 65–81, Wm. B. Eerdmans Publishing Company, 1949. A theological review: Kuyper, Abraham, *Principles of Sacred Theology*, pp. 397–563, Wm. B. Erdmans Publishing Company, 1954.

3. The sufficiency and perspicuity of Scripture: Cunningham, William, *Theological Lectures*, pp. 447–625. Robert Carter & Brothers, 1878.

4. Inspiration and the early fathers: Westcott, B. F., *An Introduction to the Study of the Gospels*, Appendix B, 7th edition, The Macmillan Company, London, 1888; and Lee, William, *The Inspira-*

tion of Holy Scripture, Appendix G, 3d edition. Hodges, Smith & Company, Dublin, 1864.

5. Inspiration and the Reformers: Fullerton, Kemper, "Luther's Doctrine and Criticism of Scripture," in *Bibliotheca Sacra,* Vol. LXIII (1906), pp. 1–34, 284–298; Warfield, B. B., *Calvin and Calvinism,* pp. 60–70, Oxford University Press, 1931.

IV.

Hermeneutics

Hermeneutics defines the rules that one follows when searching out the meaning of Scripture. These rules are not peculiar to Christianity. They differ in language, but not in substance, from the rules that educated people follow when searching out the meaning of *any* system of thought.

The doctrines of Scripture can be apprehended only as we approach the text with a spirit of meekness. Humility before the facts is the precondition of all learning, whether of Christianity or botany. We must submit to the system.

To " submit to the system " means to be fair and honest with the manner in which the controlling concepts are related. A novel is ordered by a plot, a dictionary by alphabetical sequence. A novel should be read from the beginning; a dictionary can be opened anywhere. But in either case the system must be respected.

This is particularly true in the case of great books. The reader must immerse himself in the text; the system does not jump out at him. Melville was pleased that Hawthorne understood *Moby Dick,* for the general public missed the point.

Since the Bible is a work of art, its system is easily corrupted by the cultic mind. " So also our beloved brother Paul wrote to you according to the wisdom given him, speaking of this as he does in all his letters. There are some things in them hard to understand, which the ignorant and unstable twist to their own destruction, as they do the other scriptures." (II Peter 3:15-16.) The Bible is vulnerable to cultic thinking because it was written by no less than thirty authors, from every rank and class of society, over a span of nearly fifteen centuries.

1. *Progressive Revelation*

The concept of "progressive revelation" is the key to Biblical hermeneutics. "Revelation is not complete all at once. If the light with which it starts is dim, it grows clearer as the ages advance. The world into which it comes is one deeply sunk in sin, and in the evils which sin brings with it. Revelation has to take up man as it finds him, with his crude conceptions, his childlike modes of thought and expression, his defective moral ideas and social institutions, and has to make the best of him it can. Imperfect conditions have to be borne with for the time, while germs of truth and principles are implanted which, in their development, gradually throw off the defective forms, and evolve higher."[1] For example, Lot violated parental duty by offering his daughters to be polluted. (Gen. 19:8.) His conduct was prompted, though not excused, by the sacred rites of hospitality that prevailed in Eastern nations at that time. (Cf. Judg. 19:22-24.)

Each stage of divine revelation must be interpreted from within the spiritual and cultural level of the people being addressed. "The Mosaic stage of revelation, e.g., did not clearly condemn polygamy or slavery, though it held in it . . . ideas and principles which effectively wrought for the abolition of both. The Song of Deborah is an inspired production — Deborah is a 'prophetess' — but parts are on the lower key of the rude age of the Judges. There are portions of the Psalms — prayers for the destruction of enemies and imprecatory psalms, which no Christian congregation could now sing, or use in any form without excessive spiritualization. . . . Jesus disclaims the imitation by his disciples of the example of Elijah. What was suitable to the age and circumstances of that prophet (Jesus does not condemn Elijah) might not be suitable to a higher dispensation. All this does not detract from the sufficiency of the Biblical record, taken as a whole; it detracts only from the sufficiency of certain portions of it if taken by themselves. The lower stages have to be read in the light of the higher, with the correction which the higher affords. A Christian may uphold the divine authority of the Old Testament, but he will not feel that he is bound by the Mosaic law of divorce. Jesus did not come to destroy the law or the prophets, but to fulfill them. But the fulfillment was itself an abrogation of whatever was imperfect in the earlier stages." [2]

Even the apostles had to grow in knowledge. Although Peter *prophesied* the breakdown of the wall between Jews and Gentiles, it was only after a shameful bout with pride that he conceded the very thing he prophesied. " Though this calling of the Gentiles was announced by so many testimonies, yet when the apostles were about to enter upon it, it appeared to them so novel and strange, that they dreaded it, as if it had been a prodigy: indeed it was with trepidation and reluctance that they at length engaged in it." [3]

This is clear enough. But apparently it is not clear enough for the cultic mind. Cultic thinking tends to impose a uniformity on Scripture that Scripture itself disavows. Since the Bible is plenarily inspired, the cultic mind assumes that all verses in the Bible are equally normative. No allowance is made for the part that a particular verse plays in the analogy of faith. Open the Bible anywhere, and a " promise for the day " can be claimed.

Two principles must be kept in delicate balance: *first,* the whole of Scripture is inspired; *secondly,* some parts of Scripture are subject to the illumination of other parts. If a Christian neglects the second principle, out of a zeal to honor the first, his conduct hardly conduces to healthy Biblical faith.

Five rules govern Biblical hermeneutics: *first,* the New Testament interprets the Old Testament; *secondly,* the Epistles interpret the Gospels; *thirdly,* systematic passages interpret the incidental; *fourthly,* universal passages interpret the local; *fifthly,* didactic passages interpret the symbolic. If any rule is neglected, the harmony of Scripture is disrupted.

2. *First, the New Testament Interprets the Old Testament*

Although the Abrahamic covenant is one covenant, it is administered in two economies. The Old Testament is the " economy of

preparation "; the New Testament, the "economy of fulfillment."
The Old Testament is a shadow of better things to come. (Heb.
10:1.) And since the shadow derives from the substance, the old
economy derives from the new economy. The prophets look forward
to Christ; the apostles are eyewitnesses. *Therefore, in no case does
the Old Testament enjoy primacy over the New Testament.* Moses
is a servant in the house, while Christ is the Son.

A neglect of this principle accounts for much of the present blindness in the Jewish nation. " Yes, to this day whenever Moses is read
a veil lies over their minds." (II Cor. 3:15.) Moses received his
authority from Christ, not the other way around.

Roman Catholicism is cultic when it rests its distinctives, such
as prayers for the dead, on apocryphal elements in the Septuagint
canon. It forgets that the limits of Christian theology are decided by
the New Testament, not the Old Testament.

Seventh-day Adventism is cultic when it converts an Old Testament ceremony into a New Testament principle. The apostles worshiped on the first day of the week rather than on the seventh, because the first day commemorated both the Lord's victory over
death and the Pentecostal outpouring of the Spirit. God requires a
seventh of our time; that is the principle. The day in the week is the
ceremony. The apostles kept the principle but dropped the ceremony. Seventh-day Adventism separates itself from the church
by siding with the Jewish rather than with the Christian tradition.

Dispensationalism makes a similar mistake in eschatology. It uses
Old Testament prophecies to prove that the Jews have a theocratic
destiny outside the church. Dispensationalism forgets that prophecy
is *not* self-interpreting. When Malachi says, " Behold, I will send
you Elijah the prophet before the great and terrible day of the Lord
comes " (Mal. 4:5), no exegesis of the Old Testament would sug-
gest that Malachi spoke of John the Baptist. Yet, Jesus assures us
that John *was* the object of this prophecy. (Matt. 11:14; 17:9-13.)
" It should be remembered that it is part of the character of the
Scripture prophecies not to be so framed as to be fully understood
before the event. . . . 'Prophecy is *not to be its own interpreter*';
that is, is not to have its full sense made out (like that of any other

kind of composition) by the study of the very words of each prophecy itself, but it is to be interpreted by the event that fulfills it." [4] The degree to which prophecy is typical or literal is decided by the theology of the New Testament. "As to the restoration of the Jews and of Jerusalem, many indeed and glorious are the promises to this effect which are found in Scripture, but they are not so numerous, nor so strongly expressed as the declarations of the everlasting duration of the Mosaic law; and *these,* all Christians are agreed, must be understood, not literally, but figuratively and spiritually." [5]

Cultic thinking often crops up where one would least expect it. For example, Matthew Henry tried to justify seventeenth-century laws on witchcraft by an appeal to the Old Testament. "By our law consulting, covenanting with, invocating, or employing, any evil spirit, to any intent whatsoever, and exercising any enchantment, charms, sorcery, whereby hurt shall be done to any person whatsoever, is made felony, without benefit of clergy; also pretending to tell where goods lost or stolen may be found, or the like, is an iniquity punishable by the judge and the second offense with death. The justice of our law herein, is supported by the law of God here." [6] This confidence is misdirected, for the Mosaic laws against witchcraft perished with the old economy.

Cultic thinking also tinctures the classical theologies. For example, Calvinism seldom appreciates the extent to which the New Testament ethic judges the truncated ethic of the Old Testament. Although Jesus plainly says, "*A new commandment* I give to you, that you love one another" (John 13:34), Calvinism judges the law of love as nothing but a religious summary of the Ten Commandments. "The Ten Commandments are summed up by Christ into these two: Thou shalt love the Lord thy God with all thy heart, and soul, and might; and thou shalt love thy neighbor as thyself." [7] This is an erroneous judgment, for the Ten Commandments do not take in Christ's active obedience. Christ is righteous because he loved with perfection, not because he eschewed murder and theft. Whereas the Ten Commandments negate, love affirms. Moses gave *form* to the law of love (Lev. 19:18; Deut. 6:5), but only Christ could give it *substance.*

The New Testament abrogates everything that does not materially advance the Abrahamic covenant. When the Pharisees inquired about the Mosaic law of divorce, they were told that the law was written for their " hardness of heart " and that it was contrary to the creative order. (Mark 10:2-6.) The same can be said about slavery. The Jews could make slaves of other people, but not of fellow Jews (Lev. 25:39 ff.); capital punishment was enforced, but not against a man who killed a slave (Ex. 21:20-21). This ethic, in and of itself, is no higher than that of Plato and Aristotle. And the New Testament stands in judgment on it, for the law of love negates any static subordination of life to life. Human equality is the limiting concept of all Christian social action.

The Old Testament authorized the congregation to stone a rebellious son (Deut. 21:18-21), but the New Testament confers the power of the sword on the civil magistrate alone (Rom. 13:1-7). The church has no jurisdiction in temporal affairs.

Even so disturbing an incident as the Amalekite massacre is mitigated by the concept of progressive revelation. Since Israel's battle tactics shared in the standards of cruelty that prevailed at that time, no mercy was shown (I Sam. 15:3). It was for their " hardness of heart " that God used these standards in the service of his will, for Jesus lists mercy among the " weightier matters " of the law. And by law he means the Mosaic law.

It is important to observe, however, that the New Testament *fulfills* the Old Testament; it does not reject it. The Old Testament is a storehouse of instruction because it adumbrates the New Testament. " Now these things happened to them as a warning, but they were written down for our instruction, upon whom the end of the ages has come." (I Cor. 10:11.) The principles in the Old Testament are eternal; their mode of administration is temporal. God used fire from heaven to reveal his displeasure with unbelief. The displeasure is eternal; the use of fire is temporal. "During that period, in which he gave the Israelites his covenant involved in some degree of obscurity, he intended to signify and prefigure the grace of future and eternal felicity by terrestrial blessings, and the grievousness of spiritual death by corporal punishments." [8]

3. *Secondly, the Epistles Interpret the Gospels*

In liturgical churches it is customary for the laity to rise when the Gospel is read, while remaining seated when the Epistle is read. This is cultic, for it implies that the Gospels are entitled to more reverence than the Epistles. But we are assured, on very clear evidence, that the fullness of revelation came *after* the Gospels. " I have yet many things to say to you, but you cannot bear them now. When the Spirit of truth comes, he will guide you into all the truth." (John 16:12-13.)

The Synoptic Gospels contain a few very cryptic elements. These elements are easily corrupted by the cultic mind. Jesus said it is better to mutilate the body than to go to hell (Mark 9:43-47); zealots gouge out their eyeballs. Jesus said that some are made eunuchs for the Kingdom's sake (Matt. 19:12); Origen castrated himself. Jesus spoke of spiritual powers without telling whether these powers could be claimed by future generations (Luke 10:19); the Dolly Pond cult handle venomous snakes as a proof of faith. Jesus reviewed the Last Times without distinguishing between the destruction of Jerusalem and the events accompanying his own return (Matt., ch. 24); the Anabaptists set up an earthly kingdom. Jesus forbade his disciples to take an oath or resist an evil person (ch. 5:33-42); Tolstoy constructed a lofty social ethic which disregarded the distinction between personal and official conduct.

Jesus did not develop a systematic theology for at least two reasons. *First,* a normative interpretation of his life, death, and resurrection could not be given until these events had actually happened; *secondly,* the Holy Spirit could not be sent in the *name* of Jesus until that name had been earned. (John 7:39.) Jesus completed the Old Testament while he ushered in the New Testament; he submitted to the ceremonial law that he might have a base from which to terminate the ceremonial law. But Jesus did *not* connect his own Messianic office with the promises made to Abraham. This work was bequeathed to the disciples. For example, when Jesus told the rich young ruler to sell his possessions (Mark 10:17-22), or when he depicted scenes from the Final Judgment (Matt. 25:31-46), he implied that sinners are justified by works. This seems to conflict with

Paul's teaching that sinners are justified by faith (Rom. 4:16-25). But the conflict exists in the cultic mind, for it was never Jesus' intention to develop a systematic theology.

This principle is often offended. When the liturgical churches read, "Truly, truly, I say to you, unless one is born of water and the Spirit, he cannot enter the kingdom of God" (John 3:5), they promptly conclude that Jesus is teaching baptismal regeneration. The conclusion is cultic. If a Christian wants to settle the relation between baptism and regeneration, he must turn to passages that have this question in view; and the Lord's discourse with Nicodemus is *not* one of these passages. Nor is the discourse on the "bread of life" (ch. 6:25-59) a relevant base from which to defend the medieval view of the Eucharist.

4. *Thirdly, Systematic Passages Interpret the Incidental*

Though all parts of the Bible are connected with the Abrahamic covenant, not all parts are *directly* connected; for it is only as we reach the systematic sections of the Epistles that a theological effort is made to trace the relation between this covenant and Christ's Messianic office. Christ is the federal head of a new and holy race; he invested human nature with perfection by loving God with all his heart and his neighbor as himself. The human nature was then offered on the cross to satisfy divine justice. Being propitious toward the world, God forgives all who repent. This is the gospel, and its nerve center is justification by faith.

There are only two places in Scripture where justification is treated in a systematic, didactic form. These are Romans and Galatians. This does not mean that justification is concealed elsewhere, for God's Word is one. Abraham was justified by faith, even as we are. It only means that justification is *implied* in some places, while in others it is *systematically developed*. Paul touches on justification in Phil. 3:6 ff., Titus 3:5 ff., and elsewhere; but it is characteristic of Paul not to return to a subject that he has treated at length in a particular epistle or group of epistles. John develops the plan of salvation; so does the book of Hebrews. But only Romans and Galatians make a didactic effort to connect the blessings of the covenant with the gift of God's Son. *Therefore, if the church teaches anything that offends the system of Romans and Galatians, it is cultic.*

Since the concept of progressive revelation touches all portions of the Bible, however, not everything in the Epistles is systematic. For example, Paul speaks of "baptism for the dead" in a highly doctrinal chapter (I Cor. 15:29). The import of this passage is admittedly obscure. But theology is not affected, whatever the import may be, for theology draws on systematic, not incidental passages. Mormonism is cultic when it elevates proxy baptism to a cardinal doctrine. If there were any connection between baptism for the dead and the Abrahamic covenant, Paul would have reviewed this in Romans and Galatians.

But the cults do not have a monopoly on the cultic mentality. For example, Baptists often limit fellowship to those who have been immersed. This is unfortunate. If the mode of baptism had any connection with the Abrahamic covenant, Paul would have reviewed this in Romans and Galatians. The same can be said about the Lutheran view of the real presence, the Anglican view of succession, and the Methodist view of subjective holiness.

Liturgical churches place considerable emphasis on the rite of baptism itself. This is cultic, for Romans and Galatians name *faith,* not baptism, as the instrumental cause of justification.

Roman Catholicism sees the cultic elements in Protestantism, but not in Roman Catholicism. Yet, the theology of Mary rests on data that are not even found in Scripture. The appeal is to "unwritten tradition." But if there were any connection between the Abrahamic covenant and the intercessory work of Mary, Paul would have reviewed this in Romans and Galatians. We look in vain for any such connection.

Roman Catholicism says we are saved by what we *do,* not by what we *believe;* and in saying this it appeals to what looks like very clear evidence: "You see that a man is justified by works and not by faith alone" (James 2:24). But James is correcting an abuse of faith; he is not developing the plan of salvation. He says that when faith is *alone,* not having good works, it is not vital faith at all. Paul says the same thing: "For it is not the hearers of the law who are

righteous before God, but the doers of the law who will be justified "
(Rom. 2:13). Whenever profession does not issue in a lively sense of
charity, it stands condemned. " We never dream either of a faith
destitute of good works, or of a justification unattended by them:
this is the sole difference, that while we acknowledge a necessary
connection between faith and good works, we attribute justification,
not to works, but to faith." [9]

Roman Catholicism defends the sacrament of extreme unction
by an appeal to the oil passage in James (ch. 5:14-15). But the appeal is cultic, for James is talking about *sick*, not dying, people.
Furthermore, if anointing with oil had any connection with the
Abrahamic covenant, Paul would have reviewed this in Romans
and Galatians.

Roman Catholicism prefers James above Paul. In doing so, however, it egregiously offends right procedure. " When there is an appearance of repugnancy or contradiction in any places of Scripture,
if some, or any of them, do treat directly, designedly, and largely
about the matter concerning which there is a seeming repugnancy or
contradiction; and others, or any other, speak of the same things
only ' obiter,' occasionally, transiently, in order unto other ends; the
truth is to be learned, stated, and fixed from the former places: or
the interpretation of those places where any truth is mentioned only
occasionally with reference unto other things or ends, is, as unto that
truth, to be taken from and accommodated unto those other places
wherein it is the design and purpose of the holy penman to declare
it *for its own sake,* and to guide the faith of the church therein. . . .
According unto this rule, it is unquestionable that the doctrine of
justification before God is to be learned from the writings of the
apostle Paul, and from them is light to be taken into all other places
of Scripture where it is occasionally mentioned. . . . For it must be
acknowledged that he wrote of this subject of our justification before God, on purpose to declare it for its own sake, and its use in
the church; and that he doth it fully, largely, and frequently, in a
constant harmony of expressions." [10]

The third canon of hermeneutics needs no special defense, for
it is only an extension of the kind of procedure that educated people follow when *any* system of thought is under examination. For

example, the Platonic system connects such concepts as God, the Good, the world of Ideas, the Demiurge, the theory of reminiscence, and the space-time receptacle. But not everything in the dialogues advances this system; obiter dicta are abundant. The dicta do not disturb Platonic scholars, however, for scholars have more sense than to subordinate systematic passages to incidental. If the church had exhibited a measure of this same sense, the Reformation might have been avoided.

5. Fourthly, Universal Passages Interpret the Local

Scripture often communicates universal principles through local ceremonies. But this very artistry exposes Scripture to the abusive tactics of the cultic mind. Observe, for example, the skillful manner in which Jesus taught the principle of love and humility: he washed the feet of his disciples. The principle is universal; the ceremony is local. Since foot washing has no relevance outside a culture of sand and sandals, it cannot be imposed on the church universal.

It is particularly necessary that right procedure be followed when the Epistles are studied, for not everything in the Epistles is normative. For example, Peter tells women how to adorn themselves; and his advice is remarkably precise: " Let not yours be the outward adorning with braiding of hair, decoration of gold, and wearing of robes " (I Peter 3:3). When enthusiasts cite this passage to control women's fashions, they render Christianity trivial and offensive. The apostles taught the principle of modesty through counsel which was pertinent to the culture of that day. In another culture a woman might *prove* her modesty by braided hair, decoration of gold, and wearing of robes.

The First Letter of Paul to the Corinthians contains a baffling admixture of universal and local elements, as illustrated by chapter seven. Here Paul advanced general truth by answering particular questions (v. 1); and among such questions was that of marriage. Since the church was on the eve of an "impending distress," Paul advised the postponement of wedlock (v. 26). There is a time to marry and a time to remain single. To defend perpetual celibacy on the strength of this advice is cultic.

Again, Paul tells the Corinthian women to respect the federal headship of the male by wearing a veil (I Cor. 11:2-9); and in giving this advice he appeals to existing social mores: "That is why a woman ought to have a veil on her head, because of the angels" (v. 10). When Roman Catholicism insists that women cover their heads when entering a church, it is cultic. Since Occidental societies do not require external evidence of female subordination, a modern woman honors the principle by wearing a veil over her heart.

On another occasion Paul tells Philemon how to treat a runaway slave: Philemon should be just and considerate. The principle is eternal; its application to a slave economy is circumstantial. When critics chide the apostles for not attacking the institution of slavery, they betray a very unimaginative grasp of Christian social action. The apostles attacked slavery in the same way they attacked the tyranny of Caesar — with grace and dignity, not grossly and frontally. Love is the law of life, and love stands in judgment on any static subordination of life to life. The apostles chose a subtle course because the existing order suffered from "hardness of heart." Unless social changes are introduced gradually, revolution is invited. In such a case the gospel would be identified with an ideology and the promised blessings would be obscured, if not destroyed altogether.

Pentecostalism tries to revive the charismatic gifts, but it does not reckon with the economy that made these gifts necessary. Speaking in tongues served as a public demonstration of the Holy Spirit's presence among the Gentiles: "For they heard them speaking in tongues and extolling God. Then Peter declared, 'Can any one forbid water for baptizing these people who have received the Holy Spirit just as we have?'" (Acts 10:46-47). When the wall of partition between Jews and Gentiles was demolished, the charismatic gifts yielded to love as the "more excellent way" (I Cor. 12:31). Paul delineates this more excellent way in his later Epistles; reference to the charismatic gifts vanishes. Whereas love edifies, speaking in tongues can be enlisted in the service of pride.

Some may object that a precise line cannot be drawn between universal and local elements in the New Testament. The objection is valid, but irrelevant. A line *must* be drawn; the task is not op-

tional. For example, Paul says, " Greet one another with a holy kiss."
(Rom. 16:16.) This is a command; it is apostolical; and it falls within
the book of Romans. Yet, there is only one way in which the church
can honor this command, and that is by distinguishing between the
principle of Christian fraternity and the first-century ceremony of
a holy kiss.

The fourth rule of hermeneutics may explain why some of Paul's
letters are not in the canon. While no final proof is possible, the
missing letters may have been too local in character to profit the
church universal.

6. *Fifthly, Didactic Passages Interpret the Symbolic*

Some sections of the New Testament are systematic in form,
though symbolic in substance. The Olivet discourse and the book of
Revelation are the most prominent examples. In such cases the symbols must be illuminated by didactic passages, for symbols share in
the general limitations of Biblical prophecy. Prophecy, let us remember, is *not* its own interpreter. Whereas didactic language is
open and plain, symbols are shadowy and ambiguous.

The fifth rule of hermeneutics is a functional extension of the first
rule. *Just as the Old Testament is subject to the New Testament,
so the symbolic passages in the New Testament are subject to the
didactic passages; and for precisely the same reason.* To reverse this
order is cultic.

Roman Catholicism often uses Biblical symbols to sustain its
" counsels of perfection." For example, the book of Revelation implies that virginity is a better moral state than marriage: " It is these
who have not defiled themselves with women, for they are chaste "
(ch. 14:4). But moral theology must look to passages that have moral
theology in view, and the book of Revelation is *not* one of these
passages. Love is the law of life, and love enjoins an equal obligation on all men, factory worker and monk alike. Whether a person
marries or remains single depends upon the call of God.

Dispensationalism uses Biblical symbols to defend a pretribula-
tion view of the rapture. But if the church were to be raptured before the tribulation, Paul would have taught this in First and Sec-

ond Thessalonians. In these Epistles he traces the events of the Last Times in plain, didactic language; and he says that the hope of the church is the return of Christ, not deliverance from tribulation (II Thess. 2:1-12).

Dispensationalism is anxious to have the church raptured in order that an earthly Semitic kingdom might be founded. But this anxiety is fathered by a capital theological error. Unless the future of saved Jews falls within the general life of the church, we replace the spirit of the gospel with the spirit of Old Testament Judaism. " Now if all these things were to come to pass, the determined expectation of which caused the Jews to reject Christ — if he should actually appear, with miraculous splendor, as the restorer of the Jewish nation, and city, and Temple, reigning over the whole world as a great earthly sovereign, and reserving peculiar privileges for his own nation — if, I say, all these expectations should be fulfilled, to which the Jews have so long and so obstinately clung, surely this would not be so much a conversion of the Jews to Christianity, as *a conversion of Christians to Judaism;* it would not be bringing the Jews to the gospel by overcoming their national prejudices but rather carrying back the gospel to meet the Jewish prejudices; it would be destroying the spiritual character of our religion, and establishing those erroneous views which have hitherto caused the Jews to reject it. We may conclude, then, that all the promises and predictions in Scripture relative to the future glories of the Jews and of Jerusalem, are to be understood of the Christian church, of which the Jewish church was a figure; and all that is said of feasting, and splendor, and wealth, and worldly greatness and enjoyment, is to be interpreted spiritually of the inward comfort and peace of mind, and ' joy of the Holy Ghost ' (I Thessalonians i.6), which is promised to sincere Christians in this life, and of the unspeakable happiness prepared for them after death." [11]

COLLATERAL READING

1. Progressive revelation and Biblical authority: Hannah, J., *The Relation Between the Divine and Human Elements in Holy Scripture* (Bampton Lectures, 1863), pp. 74-106, J. Murray, London, 1863.

2. The harmony of Paul and James: Barrows, E. P., " The Alleged Disagreement Between Paul and James," in *Bibliotheca Sacra,* Vol. IX (1852), pp. 761–782; Calvin, *Institutes,* III. xvii. 11–13; John Owen, *Works* (Wm. Goold, ed.), Vol. V, pp. 384–400, T. & T. Clark, Edinburgh, 1862.

3. Legalism in Calvinistic ethics: Murray, John, *Principles of Conduct,* Wm. B. Eerdmans Publishing Company, 1957. Love has no content (pp. 19–26); men *must* work six days a week (pp. 82–89); slavery is not intrinsically wrong (pp. 92–106). Topics such as " mercy " and " tragic moral choice " are not even treated.

4. James and the anointing with oil: Warfield, B. B., *Miracles: Yesterday and Today,* pp. 169–173, Wm. B. Eerdmans Publishing Company, 1953.

5. The charismatic gifts: Kuyper, Abraham, *The Work of the Holy Spirit,* pp. 133–138, Wm. B. Eerdmans Publishing Company, 1946; John Owen, *Works* (Wm. Goold, ed.), Vol. IV, pp. 438–486, T. & T. Clark, Edinburgh, 1862; Warfield, B. B., *Miracles: Yesterday and Today,* pp. 3–31, Wm. B. Eerdmans Publishing Company, 1953.

6. Standard sources for classical premillennialism: Gill, John, *A Body of Doctrinal Divinity,* Book VII, Ch. VIII; Reese, Alexander, *The Approaching Advent of Christ,* Marshall, Morgan & Scott, Ltd., London, 1937.

7. The best answer to Roman Catholicism: Salmon, George, *The Infallibility of the Church,* James D. Bales, Searcy, Ark., 1948.

V.

Theology

SINCE the entire Bible is inspired of God, the theologian must honor *all* the data of Scripture. Nothing is unimportant; nothing can be safely neglected.

This having been said, however, it yet remains true that Romans and Galatians are the highest ranking sources in theology, for they alone develop the terms of the Abrahamic covenant in systematic, didactic language. And of the two sources Romans is the more fruitful. There is a historical reason for this. When Paul wrote Romans, not only was his apostolic authority fully established, but there were no local controversies to distract his mind from the grand task of reviewing the plan of salvation. The result was a perfect treatise in systematic theology. "We have no trace here of the ultra-liberalism of Corinth, or the dreamy asceticisms of Colossae, or the servile Pharisaisms of Galatia. Clearly he is not dealing with any *special* dissensions, heresies, or attacks on his authority. The very value of the Epistle, as a systematic exposition of 'the Gospel of Protestantism,' depends on the calmness and lucidity with which the apostle appeals to an ideal public to follow him in the discussion of abstract truths." [1]

1. *The Gospel and the Wrath of God*

The subject of theology is the gospel: " The gospel concerning his Son, who was descended from David according to the flesh and designated Son of God in power according to the Spirit of holiness by his resurrection from the dead, Jesus Christ our Lord " (Rom.

1:3-4). Since the price of pardon was paid by Christ on the cross, and since Christ offered himself out of love, the gospel reveals both the justice and the mercy of God — justice because God is righteous in his very nature, and mercy because God has resources of pity that transcend the strict demands of law.

Unless the gospel is spiritually perceived, it is not perceived at all, for an offer of mercy would hardly attract an individual who denied his need of mercy. The wrath of God makes mercy relevant by creating judicial fear in the heart. " For the wrath of God is revealed from heaven against all ungodliness and wickedness of men who by their wickedness suppress the truth." (V. 18.) To "suppress the truth " means to enlist the law of God in the service of pride. Sinners judge one another by a standard that they themselves fail to keep. "Therefore you have no excuse, O man, whoever you are, when you judge another; for in passing judgment upon him you condemn yourself, because you, the judge, are doing the very same things." (Ch. 2:1.)

Sinners do not *become* sinners when they sin; they sin because they are sinners. Paul proves this by locating sin in the will and in the affections: " There is no fear of God before their eyes " (ch. 3:18). It is of the very essence of sin to prefer the self before God. " By *sin,* in this case, cannot be understood actual sin. It must mean indwelling sin, or corruption of nature; sin as the principle or source of action, and not as an act. . . . That is, from sin immanent in our nature, comes first desire, and then the act." [2] Sin either imagines that man is the author of his own moral standards, or that if the standards derive from God, man is rightly related to them. The law shatters this pretense. "Law came in, to increase the trespass." (Ch. 5:20.) The law disarms a sinner by revealing both the fact and the seriousness of sin. " Now we know that whatever the law says it speaks to those who are under the law, so that every mouth may be stopped, and the whole world may be held accountable to God." (Ch. 3:19.) " The law, although it cannot secure either the justification or sanctification of men, performs an essential part in the economy of salvation. It enlightens conscience, and secures its verdict against a multitude of evils, which we should not otherwise have recognized as sins. It arouses sin, increasing its power, and making it, both in itself and in our consciousness, exceedingly sinful. It therefore produces that state of mind which is a necessary preparation for the reception of the gospel." [3]

2. *The Righteousness of God*

While the law clarifies sin, it does not clarify salvation. Only the gospel can undertake this better task: " But now the righteousness of God has been manifested apart from law, although the law and the prophets bear witness to it, the righteousness of God through faith in Jesus Christ for all who believe " (vs. 21-22). Christ assumed human nature that he might become the progenitor of a new and holy race. By loving God with all his heart and his neighbor as himself, he invested human nature with perfection. *This is Christ's active obedience.* In the fullness of time he propitiated the offended judicial sentiment in God by offering up his life as a living sacrifice on the cross. *This is Christ's passive obedience.* The gospel is the good news that God offers a full pardon to all who repent. Sinners are justified " through the redemption which is in Christ Jesus, whom God put forward as an expiation [propitiation] by his blood, to be received by faith " (vs. 24-25).

It was on the express authority of this teaching that the Reformers took their stand against the legalism of the Roman church. " The Reformers taught that, when God pardoned and accepted any sinner, the ground or basis of the divine act — *that* to which God had directly and immediately a respect or regard in performing it, or in passing a virtual sentence canceling that man's sins, and admitting him into the enjoyment of his favor — was this, that the righteousness of Christ was his, through his union to Christ; that being his in this way, it was in consequence imputed to him, or put down to his account, just as if it were truly and properly his own; and that this righteousness, being in itself fully satisfactory and meritorious, formed an adequate ground on which his sins might be forgiven and his person accepted." [4]

Unless we perceive that Christ satisfied divine justice, we miss the very essence of the gospel. " This was to show God's righteousness, because in his divine forbearance he had passed over former sins; it was to prove at the present time that he himself is righteous and that he justifies him who has faith in Jesus." (Vs. 25-26.) Christ vicariously bore the punishment due to sinners: "God made [us] alive together with him, having forgiven us all our trespasses, having canceled the bond which stood against us with its legal demands; this he set aside, nailing it to the cross" (Col. 2:13-14). "If Christ had merely died a corporeal death, no end would have been accomplished by it; it was requisite, also, that he should feel the severity of the divine vengeance, in order to appease the wrath of God, and satisfy his justice. Hence it was necessary for him to contend with the powers of hell and the horror of eternal death. We have already stated from the prophet, that 'the chastisement of our peace was upon him,' that 'he was wounded for our transgressions, and bruised for our iniquities'; . . . the meaning of which is, that he was made a substitute and surety for transgressors, and even treated as a criminal himself, to sustain all the punishments which would have been inflicted on them; only with this exception, that 'it was not possible that he should be holden of the pains of death.'"[5]

When sinners imagine that God will overlook the consequences of transgression, they operate on a principle lower than that of general society. We do not and we cannot have fellowship with those who violate our dignity. Whenever we are offended, the judicial sentiment is aroused; and it stays aroused until right moral conditions prevail. The offending party must either apologize or repent, depending on the situation. To grant this in the case of man, but to deny it in the case of God, what is this but to deny that God is good?

3. Justification

Since Christ propitiated the offended judicial sentiment in God, repentant sinners are clothed with the garments of forgiveness. They are righteous in God's eyes; and being righteous, they are declared so. " Therefore, since we are justified by faith, we have peace with God through our Lord Jesus Christ." (Rom. 5:1.) " By justification we mean — man's acceptance with God, or his being regarded and treated as righteous in his sight — as the object of his favor, and not of his wrath; of his blessing, and not of his curse." [6] To *declare* a sinner righteous does not *constitute* him righteous. " The word *justify* . . . means to reckon, or pronounce, or declare righteous, or to resolve on treating as righteous; and the justification of a sinner, therefore, is descriptive of a change effected by an act of God, not upon his moral character, but upon his state or condition in relation to the law under which he was placed, and to God, the author and the guardian of that law — a change whereby he who is the object of it ceases to be held or reckoned and treated as guilty, and liable to punishment — has a sentence of acquittal and approbation pronounced upon him — is forgiven all his past offenses, and is admitted into the enjoyment of God's favor and friendship." [7]

When Christians wonder how believers in the old economy were saved, they reverse the true order of the problem. Paul says we *know* how they were saved. The hope of the church is that we are saved in precisely the same way: " For what does the scripture say? ' Abraham believed God, and it was reckoned to him as righteousness.' . . . That is why it depends on faith, in order that the promise may rest on grace and be guaranteed to all his descendants — not only to the adherents of the law but also to those who share the faith of Abraham, for he is the father of us all, as it is written, ' I have made you the father of many nations ' " (ch. 4:3-17).

Positional righteousness evokes the easy objection that we may continue in sin, and yet enjoy the prospects of heaven. Paul anticipates this objection: " What shall we say then? Are we to continue in sin that grace may abound? By no means! How can we who died to sin still live in it? Do you not know that all of us who have been baptized into Christ Jesus were baptized into his death? " (ch. 6:1-3). The objection fails to see that love is a duty — though it is a duty that is unfettered by law. " And do these objectors mean to say that, because God has redeemed us from the curse of the law, therefore we *owe* him nothing, we have no *duty* now to him? Has not redemption rather made us *doubly debtors*? We *owe* him more than ever: we owe his holy law more than ever; more honor, more obedience. Duty has been *doubled,* not *canceled,* by our being delivered from the law; and he who says that *duty* has ceased, because deliverance has come, knows nothing of duty, or law, or deliverance." [8] In sum, we are free from an obedience to law as the condition of justification; the law does not prescribe the terms of our acceptance with God.

Some may object that God cannot declare sinners righteous, when they are not, in fact, righteous. The objection forgets that repentant sinners *are* righteous; their righteousness is as much a part of history as trees and clouds. Christ satisfied the terms of divine justice, and Christ richly dwells in all who believe. "For our sake he made him to be sin who knew no sin, so that in him we might become the righteousness of God." (II Cor. 5:21.) Repentant sinners are simultaneously righteous and unrighteous. They are righteous by reason of their mystical union with Christ; while in themselves, considered apart from Christ, they are unrighteous. The validity of this construction will be acknowledged by all careful students of jurisprudence. " A man may . . . be just and unjust, righteous and unrighteous at the same time. A criminal who has satisfied the demands of justice, is just in the eye of the law; he cannot be again or further punished for his offense, and is entitled to all his rights as a citizen, although morally unrighteous. The sinner, and every sinner whom God accepts or pronounces righteous for the righteousness of Christ, feels himself to be in his own person most unrighteous. God's judgment, in pronouncing him righteous, is nonetheless according to truth. He does not pronounce the sinner subjectively righteous, which he is not, but forensically righteous, which he is, because Christ has satisfied the demands of justice on his behalf." [9]

4. *Federal Headship*

Paul says that a sinner's relation to God is decided by his relation to a federal head. A federal head is an official representative; he acts in the stead of another. And Scripture names two federal heads of the human race: the " first Adam " represented the interests of mankind before the Fall; the " last Adam " represented the interests of mankind after the Fall.

The first Adam brought sin and death on the human race by violating his covenantal probation. " Therefore as sin came into the world through one man and death through sin, and so death spread to all men because all men sinned . . ." (Rom. 5:12.) Children are born with self-centered affections; they are totally depraved. " The great fact in the apostle's mind was, that God regards and treats all men, from the first moment of their existence, as out of fellowship with himself, as having forfeited his favor. . . . Here is a form of death which the violation of the law of Moses, the transgression of the law of nature, the existence of innate depravity, separately or combined, are insufficient to account for. Its infliction is antecedent to them all; and yet it is of all evils the essence and the sum. Men begin to exist out of communion with God. This is the fact which no sophistry can get out of the Bible or the history of the world. Paul tells us why it is. It is because we fell in Adam; it is for the one offense of ONE MAN that all thus die." [10] Total depravity does not mean that sinners are as bad as they can be; nor does it mean that they are incapable of general goodness. It means, *first,* that sinners have no natural affection for God; *secondly,* that they cannot remedy this defect by resident moral powers. They can only vent pride and selfishness on new and more refined levels. " That which is born of the flesh is flesh." (John 3:6.)

Jesus Christ is the last Adam; he honored the terms of his covenantal probation. By his " one act of righteousness " he rendered God propitious toward the world, thus making it possible for God to pardon all who repent. Paul sums this up in one of the profoundest passages in Scripture: " If, because of one man's trespass, death reigned through that one man, much more will those who receive the abundance of grace and the free gift of righteousness reign in life through the one man Jesus Christ. Then as one man's trespass led to condemnation for all men, so one man's act of righteousness leads to acquittal and life for all men. For as by one man's disobedience many were made sinners, so by one man's obedience many will be made righteous " (Rom. 5:17-19). This is a grand a fortiori argument. If evil came through the transgression of the first federal head — and that a ceremonial transgression — how much more will good come through the material righteousness of Jesus Christ? "Paul does not mean to say, that as Adam was the source, or cause of corruption, so Christ is the cause of holiness; but as the offense of the one was the ground of our condemnation, so the righteousness of the other is the ground of our justification." [11]

Not all men know Christ after the flesh, but all men have some knowledge of the law of God. The Jews have the oracles (ch. 3:1-2), while the Gentiles have the law written on their hearts (ch. 2:12-16). Since the law creates a consciousness of sin, God may justly command all men to repent.

5. Sanctification

A large part of the New Testament is aimed at inspiring holiness in Christians. "I appeal to you therefore, brethren, by the mercies of God, to present your bodies as a living sacrifice, holy and acceptable to God, which is your spiritual worship." (Ch. 12:1.) The first act of sanctification is regeneration, while the last act is confirmation in righteousness by the resurrection of the body. Between these two extraordinary acts a Christian grows in grace by worship, the Word, the sacraments, self-denial, and a general life of charity.

Sanctification does not mean that a believer keeps the law or performs good works. These achievements, if acceptable to God, are *fruits* of holiness. Sanctification is "*the immediate work of God by his Spirit upon our whole nature, proceeding from the peace made for us by Jesus Christ, whereby, being changed into his likeness, we are kept entirely in peace with God, and are preserved unblamable, or in a state of gracious acceptation with him, according to the terms of the covenant, unto the end.*" [12] The emphasis is on the creative work of the Spirit; we grow in grace by letting Christ come to maturity in us. "To be sanctified . . . *means to have Christ obtain stature in us. . . .* It is the reflection of Christ's form upon the mirror-surface of the soul; first in dim outlines, gradually more distinct, until the experienced eye recognizes in it the form of Jesus. But even in the most advanced it is never more than a *daguerreotype;*

Immanuel's *perfect image* will be revealed in us only in and through death." [13]

Roman Catholicism merges justification and sanctification, but this does not have the hallmark of Scripture. Justification is declaratory; sanctification is constitutive. Justification takes place once; sanctification is a lifelong process. Justification is a change in the sinner's relation to God; sanctification is a change in the sinner himself. Justification is objective; sanctification is subjective. Justification is an act done for us; sanctification is an act done in us.

Perfectionists offend Scripture when they say that indwelling sin can be eradicated by a baptism of the Holy Spirit or a second work of grace. At least three separate mistakes are made. *First,* there is a defective view of law. The law requires man to love God with all his heart and his neighbor as himself; and not to do so is sin. But no sensitive Christian can confront this task without crying with Isaiah, " Woe is me! " *Secondly,* there is a defective view of sin. Perfectionists identify sin with *conscious* sin. But relief from conscious sin is not necessarily a sign of virtue, for the relief may trace to a bad memory. " There are, in general, few stronger indications of ignorance of the power and evil of sin than the confident assertion of our ability to resist and subdue it." [14] When David cried, " Clear thou me from hidden faults " (Ps. 19:12), he testified to the deceitfulness of the human heart. It was in a similar mood that Paul cried: " I am not aware of anything against myself, but I am not thereby acquitted. It is the Lord who judges me " (I Cor. 4:4). The glory of God, not subjective feeling, is the true norm of righteousness. *Thirdly,* perfectionists believe that sanctification comes by spiritual acts of faith, whereas it comes by patient co-operation with the means of grace. We must run the race; we must die daily unto sin. Though deliverance from *law* is instantaneous, deliverance from the *law of sin* is a gradual process. " Every believer in the blood of Christ holds ' perfect sanctification,' in the sense of every believer being ' a saint,' a ' sanctified ' one; one set apart for God and his service, by the sprinkling of the blood, from the moment he believes. But perfect sanctification, in the sense of perfect freedom from sin, from the moment of believing, is nowhere taught in Scripture." [15]

6. *The Principle of Double Fulfillment*

It is important that Christians define the ground of their hope. Otherwise, they may feign a perfection that they do *not* have, or they may fail to rest in a perfection which they *do* have. Judged by law, they are imperfect; whereas judged by love, they are perfect. The difference is in the criterion.

This difference can easily be illustrated. Suppose a father wants to be kind to his children, though he ends up being unkind. Judged by law, he stands condemned; whereas judged by love, he is acquitted. The father tells his children he is sorry, and with this word they are appeased. His sorrow is a sign of love, and love seeks nothing but evidences of love.

Paul puts a similar construction on his own life. After discovering that the regenerate self pledges heights of perfection that the involved self fails to meet, Paul consoles himself by the manner in which the redeemed elements in his life despise the unredeemed elements: " I do not understand my own actions. For I do not do what I want, but I do the very thing I hate. Now if I do what I do not want, I agree that the law is good. So then it is no longer I that do it, but sin which dwells within me " (Rom. 7:15-17). Paul's hatred of evil proves that his dominant affections are inclined to righteousness. " The things which I do, when contrary to the characteristic desires and purposes of my heart, are to be considered as the acts of a slave. They are indeed my own acts, but not being performed with the full and joyful purpose of the heart, are not to be regarded as a fair criterion of character." [16]

The principle of double fulfillment is beautifully illustrated in the life of Peter. Although Peter thrice denied the Lord, his heinous sin is never mentioned again. And there is a theological reason for this silence. After Peter sinned, he went out and wept bitterly. His tears proved that he loved Christ, and love seeks nothing but evidences of love.

An oversight of this principle betrayed the Roman Catholic Church into its highly legal conception of " second justification." When the liberty of love is lost, the bondage of law re-enters. Mary and the saints must assist the sinner in his perilous journey to heaven.

Christians seldom appreciate the relation between a hatred of the carnal self in Romans, ch. 7, and the assurance of judicial release in Romans, ch. 8. All too often an artificial barrier is raised between these two chapters — as if Romans, ch. 8, sounds a victorious note that is missing in Romans, ch. 7. This sort of exegesis is manifestly inaccurate. The historical self, the self on the plane of time — this self *is* carnal. Paul's analysis of the regenerate life is normative for the church: " I am carnal, sold under sin " (ch. 7:14). " Every Christian can adopt the language of this verse. Pride, coldness, slothfulness, and other feelings which he disapproves and hates are, day by day, reasserting their power over him. He struggles against their influence, groans beneath their bondage, longs to be filled with meekness, humility, and all other fruits of the love of God, but finds he can neither of himself, nor by the aid of the law, effect his freedom from what he hates, or the full performance of what he desires and approves. Every evening witnesses his penitent confession of his degrading bondage, his sense of utter helplessness, and his longing desire for aid from above. He is a slave looking and longing for liberty." [17]

Christians miss the connection between Romans, chs. 7 and 8, because they miss the principle upon which Paul reasons. When a Christian hates the sin that dwells within him, he shows that he is born again. The Christian " is a new creature, because he has now *a new experience,* and especially *a new conflict* in his soul . . . betwixt the law in his members and the law of his mind. There is a conflict of which an unconverted man may be conscious — I mean the conflict betwixt sin and the conscience; but a new conflict begins when he is born again, and that is a conflict betwixt sin and the will. The difference betwixt the two consists entirely in the position of the will. In the former, the will is on the side of sin, and both are opposed to the conscience; in the other, the will is on the side of conscience, and both are opposed to sin. This may be said to be the characteristic difference betwixt the converted and the unconverted — both are subject to an inward conflict, but the one is willing to side with conscience, the other is willing to side with sin. When the will is made to change its position — when it is brought off from

its alliance with sin, and ranges itself on the same side with conscience and God — the great change is wrought; there may be, there
will be a conflict still; for 'there is a law in the members warring
against the law of the mind,' and our whole life must be a warfare;
and this conflict may be severe, and arduous, and protracted — inso-
much, that often the believer may be ready to exclaim, 'Oh!
wretched man that I am, who shall deliver me!' — but the very
existence of such a conflict, in which the prevailing bent and dis-
position of the will is on the side of God and holiness, is a proof
that 'we have been renewed in the Spirit of our minds,' and that
God has begun that good work in us which he will carry on unto
perfection." [18]

7. *Adoption*

The richest benefit of the gospel is enjoyed when we are adopted
into the family of God. "For all who are led by the Spirit of God are
sons of God. For you did not receive the spirit of slavery to fall back
into fear, but you have received the spirit of sonship. When we cry,
'Abba! Father!' it is the Spirit himself bearing witness with our
spirit that we are children of God." (Rom. 8:14-16.) Adoption is the
richest benefit of the gospel because it defines the state within which
all other benefits are received — filial securities in this life and con-
firmed righteousness in the life that is to come.

Since the bond between a father and his child is one of love and
not law, the child is relieved of all fear that his life is subject to constant judicial scrutiny. "There is no fear in love, but perfect love
casts out fear. For fear has to do with punishment, and he who fears
is not perfected in love." (I John 4:18.) Filial security belongs to
the very essence of adoption. If God "loved us because we loved
him, he would love us only so long as we love him, and on that
condition; and then our salvation would depend on the constancy of
our treacherous hearts. But as God loved us as sinners, as Christ
died for us as ungodly, our salvation depends . . . not on our loveli-
ness, but on the constancy of the love of God." [19]

Of course, when the child needs discipline, the father administers
it. And the discipline, at times, may be very painful. Still, the dis-

cipline is a tender expression of paternal love (Deut. 8:5; Heb. 12:5-11). God does not act as one who wounds and slays an enemy whose destruction he seeks, but as a gentle father who admonishes a son whose happiness and welfare he designs. Love is an unconditional tie. "Love bears all things, believes all things, hopes all things, endures all things." (I Cor. 13:7.) There is no perfection beyond this, whether on earth or in heaven.

The Roman Catholic Church provoked the Reformation by failing to distinguish between the law as an instrument of death and the law as an instrument of discipline. The Reformers carefully separated these two offices. Whereas the law reveals pollution and uncleanness in the Christian, it cannot render the Christian a criminal in the eyes of God. " The divine holiness in its most exalted aspect affects us, not with fear of punishment, or with anguish, because we owe a debt that we cannot pay; but with *dissatisfaction* with ourselves, with abhorrence of our uncleanness, and contempt for our righteousnesses which are as filthy rags. It makes us feel, not our *guilt,* but our *sin;* not our *condemnation,* but our hopeless *wickedness;* it does not crush us under the penalty of the law, but it causes us to be consumed by our impurity; it does not overwhelm us by righteousness, but it uncovers our unholiness and inward corruption." [20]

8. Conclusion

When Paul finishes the doctrine of adoption in Romans, ch. 8, his mind is free to range over such questions as Israel and the church, civil government, Christian liberty, and general charity. The primary task of theology is over; the plan of salvation is completed.

The theological encyclopedia is more comprehensive than the book of Romans. But when theology is wiser than Romans, it is wiser than the gospel, for Romans traces the connection between Jesus Christ and the Abrahamic covenant in systematic, didactic language. Theology may define the gospel; it may apply the gospel; but the *subject* of theology is the gospel.

COLLATERAL READING

1. The Trinity: Augustine, *On the Trinity;* Aquinas, *Summa Theologica,* I, Questions 27–43; Calvin, *Institutes,* I. xiii; Shedd, William G. T., *Dogmatic Theology,* Vol. I, pp. 249–333, Zondervan Publishing House, n.d.

2. Imputation of sin: Candlish, James Stuart, *The Biblical Doctrine of Sin,* pp. 111–122, T. & T. Clark, Edinburgh, 1893. The noetic effects of sin: Kuyper, Abraham, *Principles of Sacred Theology,* pp. 106–113, Wm. B. Eerdmans Publishing Company, 1954.

3. The necessity of the atonement: Fisk, Daniel T., " The Necessity of the Atonement," in *Bibliotheca Sacra,* Vol. XVIII (1861), pp. 284–324; Shedd, William G. T., " The Atonement, a Satisfaction for the Ethical Nature of Both God and Man," in *Bibliotheca Sacra,* Vol. XVI (1859), pp. 723–763. The theology of the atonement: Hodge, A. A., *The Atonement,* Wm. B. Eerdmans Publishing Company, 1953; Cunningham, William, *Historical Theology,* Vol. II, pp. 237–370, T. & T. Clark, Edinburgh, 1864.

4. Regeneration: Owen, John, *Works* (Wm. Goold, ed.), Vol. III, pp. 207–242, T. & T. Clark, Edinburgh, 1862; Hodge, Charles, *Essays and Reviews,* pp. 1–48, Robert Carter & Brothers, 1879.

5. Justification: Cunningham, William, *Historical Theology,* Vol. II, pp. 1–120, T. & T. Clark, Edinburgh, 1864; Hodge, Charles, *Systematic Theology,* Vol. III, pp. 114–212, Wm. B. Eerdmans Publishing Company, 1952; Bavinck, Herman, *Our Reasonable Faith,* pp. 439–468, Wm. B. Eerdmans Publishing Company, 1956.

6. Sanctification: Kuyper, Abraham, *The Work of the Holy Spirit,* pp. 432–507, Wm. B. Eerdmans Publishing Company, 1946; Candlish, James Stuart, *The Christian Salvation,* pp. 93–133, T. & T. Clark, Edinburgh, 1899. The Christian and the law of sin: Bonar, Horatius, *God's Way of Holiness,* pp. 149–166, Robert Carter & Brothers, 1870; Warfield, B. B., *Perfectionism,* 2 vols., Oxford University Press, 1931.

7. Adoption: Booth, Abraham, *The Reign of Grace,* pp. 189–198, Wm. B. Eerdmans Publishing Company, 1949; Hodge, A. A., *Out-*

lines of Theology, pp. 515–519, Wm. B. Eerdmans Publishing Company, 1949.

8. Salvation of children: Warfield, B. B., " Children," in Hastings, *Dictionary of Christ and the Gospels,* T. & T. Clark, Edinburgh, 1906.

9. Hell: Shedd, William G. T., *Dogmatic Theology,* Vol. II, pp. 667–754, Zondervan Publishing House, n.d.

VI.

Proof

WHEN JUDGED by the precision of science, the claims of religion rate low on the scale of plausibility. David Hume points this up with considerable literary eloquence: " A religionist may be an enthusiast, and imagine he sees what has no reality: he may know his narrative to be false, and yet persevere in it, with the best intentions in the world, for the sake of promoting so holy a cause: or even where this delusion has not place, vanity, excited by so strong a temptation, operates on him more powerfully than on the rest of mankind in any other circumstances; and self-interest with equal force. His auditors may not have, and commonly have not, sufficient judgment to canvass his evidence: what judgment they have, they renounce by principle, in these sublime and mysterious subjects: or if they were ever so willing to employ it, passion and a heated imagination disturb the regularity of its operations. Their credulity increases his impudence; and his impudence overpowers their credulity." [1]

A glance at the church page in a metropolitan newspaper is enough to chill the heart of any cultured person. Religious claims are so contradictory, and in many cases so downright inane, that agnosticism seems to be the only honorable refuge for an educated mind.

It is against this sort of difficulty that orthodoxy cheerfully speaks to the problem of proof. And more than this, it speaks because it is under an apostolic injunction: " In your hearts reverence Christ as Lord. Always be prepared to make a defense to any one who calls you to account for the hope that is in you, yet do it with gentleness and reverence " (I Peter 3:15).

1. *The Axiom of a Decent Society*

When orthodoxy is called on to verify its claims, it appeals to the axiom that undergirds a decent society: *namely, that in all matters where a good man is competent to judge, his word should be accepted unless sufficient reasons are found for rejecting it.* Suppose we are driving through a strange city and we want a certain address. We look for a person who seems competent and trustworthy. When this person gives us directions, we offend rectitude if we fail to act on his word. The word of a good man is assumed to be true until it is proved not true.

When we use the term "good" we mean exactly what children mean when they say that Cinderella is good. To be good means to be kind and thoughtful, and Cinderella is kind and thoughtful. Her gentle grace creates a sense of fellowship with all who are good.

When children resent Cinderella's scheming stepmother, they are prompted by three criteria: *first,* there is a difference between good and evil; *secondly,* good is better than evil; *thirdly,* good will be rewarded and evil punished.

It is on precisely these criteria that orthodoxy justifies the claims of Jesus Christ. Jesus is a good man because he verified everything that a decent society means by goodness. Not doctrinal teaching alone, not superior intellect, but a consistent exhibition of self-giving love — *this* is what holds us. Love is the substance of rectitude, and Jesus loved God with all his heart and his neighbor as himself. He healed the sick, raised the dead, comforted the sorrowing, and shed his blood for sinners. Therefore, if we can trust the word of any man, we can all the more trust the Word of Jesus Christ; for he is the absolute embodiment of whatever relative goodness we acknowledge in one another.

This conclusion can be voided only by an egregious disregard of elementary logic and morals. Either it must be proved that the axiom of a decent society is not true, or it must be proved that Jesus Christ is not a good man. The first proof, if successful, would do more than invalidate this or that decent society; it would invalidate the very *possibility* of a decent society. And the second proof can only succeed by repudiating the most firmly established evidences: " For this was not done in a corner " (Acts 26:26). Nineteen centuries of critical scholarship support the claim that Jesus Christ lived a sinless life. If we reject the goodness of Christ, despite this weight of scholarship, we court incredulity. In such a case we invalidate the possibility of *truth,* let alone a decent society.

And what is it that Christ calls on us to believe? Scripture makes this abundantly clear. We are to believe the gospel: " God so loved the world that he gave his only Son, that whoever believes in him should not perish but have eternal life " (John 3:16). The gospel is true because Jesus Christ, the Lord of the church, says it is true.

When we inquire whether Christ is competent to judge matters pertaining to salvation, we find that he is competent on the highest of all reasons. Since the Person of the Son is one with the Person of the Father, all that the Son says or does is notarized by the Father. An examination of Scripture shows that the Father's attitude toward the Son is always the same: " This is my beloved Son, with whom I am well pleased " (Matt. 3:17).

2. *The Two Routes to Faith*

At this point a serious objection must be met. Since many religious leaders fall under the heading of general goodness, how can we argue to the uniqueness of Jesus Christ? Furthermore, may not a good man be sincerely mistaken in what he believes?

The objection overlooks a critical part of the axiom in question: namely, that the word of a good man should be accepted *unless sufficient reasons are found for rejecting it.* Since the Word of Christ is harmonious with the claims of objective reality, there simply *are* no reasons for rejecting it.

This leads to a further observation. Although apologists rarely do justice to the teaching, Scripture recognizes two routes to faith. When a sincere inquirer fails to gain *direct* confidence in the Word of God, he is invited to come by way of *indirect* confidence. " If I am not doing the works of my Father, then do not believe me; but if I do them, even though you do not believe me, believe the works, that you may know and understand that the Father is in me and I am in the Father." (John 10:37-38.) Again, " Believe me that I am in the Father and the Father in me; or else believe me for the sake of the works themselves." (Ch. 14:11.) Jesus reversed the curse on nature by healing the sick, casting out demons, and raising the dead. His works are an empirical proof of his Sonship. Therefore, when a sinner believes on Christ "for the sake of the works themselves," he expresses the highest sort of faith: he believes on Christ as Lord of the new creation.

God generally asks a sinner to believe on the sheer testimony of the divine Word. But God is not a tyrant. When an inquirer makes a humble effort to compare the Word of God with claims of objective reality, God honors the effort. Since the search is for authenticity, not credibility, the veracity of God is not being called into question. The inquirer is *willing* to believe, but he finds he cannot believe until he is sure that it is God, not a preternatural counterfeit, before him. And how else can he gain this assurance, save by comparing the Word of God with the claims of objective reality?

It should be remembered, however, that unless we become as little children, we cannot believe in *any* worthy sense. " If I tell the truth, why do you not believe me? " (Ch. 8:46.) The heart must be kept tender and pliable; otherwise agnosticism converts to skepticism. In such a case the value of apologetics is voided, for apologetics is aimed at persuading doubters, not at refuting the defiant. He who demands a kind of proof that the nature of the case renders impossible, is determined that no possible evidence shall convince him.

3. *The Threat of Involuntary Unbelief*

Scripture recognizes two routes to faith because an inquirer is not always able to organize his powers of belief. In one aspect of the self he may believe, while in another aspect he may struggle with involuntary unbelief. The spirit is willing, but the flesh is weak. Under such conditions the Word of God joins forces with external evidence. For example, when Christ appeared to the disciples in his resurrected body, he did more than *say* he was their resurrected Lord. Luke makes the remarkable observation that the disciples " disbelieved for joy " (Luke 24:41). It was out of a respect for this ambivalence that Christ invited the disciples to draw near and handle him.

Even the great heroes of the faith struggled with involuntary unbelief. When the Word of God came to Gideon, it clearly said that Gideon had nothing to fear. God would go before him and win the victory. But the mission against the Midianites proved so perilous that Gideon asked for a sign. And God gave him a sign: fire sprang up from a rock and consumed the meat and unleavened cakes. But this sign was not enough, for again Gideon sought refuge in external evidence. Twice the fleece was put out, and twice God honored the test.

The crowning illustration is Abraham. When God promised Abraham a son, he used *very* clear language. Yet, Abraham was so plagued by involuntary unbelief that he entered Hagar. The Word of God returned again, and again involuntary unbelief cropped up. " Then Abraham fell on his face and laughed, and said to himself, 'Shall a child be born to a man who is a hundred years old? Shall Sarah, who is ninety years old, bear a child? '" (Gen. 17:17.) Seeking relief in external evidences, Abraham looked to Ishmael: " And Abraham said to God, 'Oh that Ishmael might live in thy sight! '" (v. 18). With this, God patiently but forcefully reiterated the substance of the promise: " No, but Sarah your wife shall bear you a son, and you shall call his name Isaac. I will establish my covenant with him as an everlasting covenant for his descendants after him " (v. 19).

Some may wonder why Abraham is called the " father of the faithful," and in particular why Paul says he did not stagger before the divine promises (Rom. 4:13-25). The answer is quite within reach. Although Abraham is the father of the faithful, this " does not imply that there was no inward conflict with doubt in Abraham's mind. It only says, that his faith triumphed over all difficulties. ' The mind,' says Calvin, ' is never so enlightened that there are no remains of ignorance, nor the heart so established that there are no misgivings. With these evils of our nature,' he adds, ' faith maintains a perpetual conflict, in which conflict it is often sorely shaken and put to great stress; but still it conquers.' " [2] The real and essential Abraham, Abraham in his dominant affections — *this* Abraham did not stagger before the promises of God. Just as Paul hated unmeet conduct, so Abraham hated impure belief; and the hatred, in each case, proved that the dominant affections were in harmony with the will of God. The principle of double fulfillment was operative. Abraham did not ask God, "How can I know thou art worthy of being trusted?" but rather, "How can I conform my trembling heart to the majesty of thy person and the wonder of thy promise?"

4. *The Lord Gives a Sign*

Since involuntary unbelief is subdued only as the Word of God joins forces with external evidence, God stands ready to give such evidence to all who humbly call on him. And this evidence is *truth*. No more effective sign can be given, for there is never a time when truth and faith are unrelated. God says, "Believe me because I am God, or else believe me because my Word is true." The route to faith is not important.

In an effort to drive home a respect for truth, God allowed false prophets to circulate in the camp of Israel. And the false prophets had much to their credit, for they predicted the future and gave signs of wonder (Deut. 13:2). But since the false prophets lacked the most important credential, the Israelites had no reason to be deceived. This missing credential was truth. The false prophets taught doctrines that were not in harmony with the redemptive events and their normative interpretation. Therefore, they stood condemned: "You shall not listen to the words of that prophet or to that dreamer of dreams; for the Lord your God is testing you, to know whether you love the Lord your God with all your heart and with all your soul" (Deut. 13:3). Whoever offends truth offends God, for God is truth.

The New Testament urges an identical principle: "Beloved, do not believe every spirit, but test the spirits to see whether they are of God; for many false prophets have gone out into the world. By this you know the Spirit of God: every spirit which confesses that Jesus Christ has come in the flesh is of God, and every spirit which does not confess Jesus is not of God" (I John 4:1-3). To deny that Christ has come in the flesh is tantamount to denying truth; for the life, death, and resurrection of Christ are as much a part of history as the exodus or the destruction of Jerusalem.

Orthodoxy has little patience with a religious pragmatism that salutes the *values* of Christ, but that fails to connect these values with the redemptive events and their normative interpretation. Unless values terminate in objective reality, we have no norm by which to distinguish the true prophet from the false. This would spell the end of theology as a science.

5. *The Meaning of Truth*

A good deal has been made of Pilate's question, "What is truth?" But the question, in truth, is artless. Just as doubt is born of confidence, so skepticism is born of truth. If Pilate had not known the meaning of truth, he could never have decided whether Christ's answer was true or false.

The cultic mind shields its distinctives by contending that religious criteria of truth are different in kind from those which educated people honor when they read a newspaper or study auto mechanics. Orthodoxy rejects this in the name of common sense and revelation. When Scripture speaks of truth, it means precisely what the man on the street means. Whether a person listens to a political speech or reads the Bible, he is called upon to judge the sufficiency of the evidences; and if he is reasonably free of prejudice, he will bring the same criteria to the one task that he does to the other.

The man on the street knows that truth is a correspondence between a thing and that which signifies it. Generally this correspondence is between a judgment and objective reality. If a person says there are twenty chairs in a room, when there are five, he does not speak the truth. But truth can also be predicated of a person. In this event the correspondence is between the total manner of his life, inward and outward, and the norm of rectitude. A true man is a good man.

Jesus is true in both senses. Since he lived a sinless life, he could predicate truth of his very person (John 14:6). But Jesus also *spoke* the truth, for his words accurately represented reality. "We worship what we know, for salvation is from the Jews." (Ch. 4:22.) The Samaritan woman believed in Jesus because he told her all that was in her heart.

Just as truth may be predicated of either a judgment or a person, so it may be conceived under two species: formal truth and material truth. *Formal truth* implies a harmony between the parts of a judgment. If a person says that all men are mortals, but denies that Socrates is a mortal, he reasons invalidly. His terms are not consistent with one another; he does not entertain formal truth.

Material truth implies a harmony between a judgment and the order of things in the real world. The parts of the judgment must be consistent with themselves and consistent with the things signified. Suppose an office window has been broken. One employee may conjecture that the damage was caused by a passing vehicle, another that it was caused by an explosion. Neither entertains material truth, for the window is too high for a passing vehicle, and the damage too slight for an explosion. But plausibility is restored when an eyewitness says that a flying bird broke the glass. And a discovery of the dead bird soon converts the hypothesis to material truth.

6. *Orthodoxy and Formal Truth*

Orthodoxy is formally true because its major doctrines are consistent with one another. God made a covenant with Abraham, and Jesus Christ is the blessing of this covenant.

Nothing would be gained by making a second review of doctrine, this time with an eye to establishing the formal truth of Scripture. The book of Romans contains a survey of Christian theology, and we have already shown that Romans is a self-consistent document.

7. *Orthodoxy and Material Truth*

Not only is orthodoxy consistent with itself, but it is consistent with the things signified. And chief among such things are the *affairs of the human heart* and the *affairs of history*. Let us briefly examine these.

When an inquirer is altogether honest with himself, he will discover two very important data: *first,* that love is the law of life (he judges inconsiderate people guilty); *secondly,* that he has insufficient moral resources to meet the terms of this law (he consistently does the very things that he condemns in others). This single discovery establishes both the uniqueness and the material truth of Scripture. *Christianity, and Christianity alone, measures the possibilities and limits of human nature by the outside criterion of self-giving love.* The Christian ethic simultaneously inspires and judges the entire human enterprise. This is a claim which deserves the most careful attention. Only the self-transcending powers of love can take in the shades of better and worse that make up the stuff of daily conduct.

All non-Christian religions construe their ethic on the optimism that the virtues of the tribe are continuous with the virtues of God. This strategy invites the furies of blood and soil by exempting the tribe from prophetic scrutiny. When selfishness is considered normal, life is subordinated to life in the name of rectitude.

I believe it was Darwin who said that were his ship to founder off some unknown island, it would be his hope that Christian missionaries had reached the island first. Everything decent traces to love, everything indecent to a lack of love. The gas chambers of Dachau are only a more frightful exhibition of man's refusal to love God with all his heart and his neighbor as himself.

Christianity not only answers to the affairs of the human heart, but it also answers to the affairs of history. And central to this history is the Jewish nation. The Jewish nation is central because the Abrahamic covenant is central.

We need not review the details of Semitic history, for these details have been established by archaeology. Orthodoxy does not say, of course, that archaeology has established *every* detail of this history. It merely says that archaeology has unearthed such an abundance of evidence that no fair-minded individual can question the material truth of Scripture. William Foxwell Albright says that the Bible is almost throughout a reliable account of historical events and a repository of original religious documents.

With the establishment of Semitic history comes the establishment of Biblical prophecy. "Prophecy is a phenomenon peculiar to Israel. Heathenism has divination, oracles, manticism; and it has been seen that divine impulse and guidance are not wholly to be refused to the wise men and teachers of other peoples. But in Israel alone we have the spectacle of a succession of men, speaking with full consciousness in the name of a holy and righteous God, maintaining a lofty and continuous testimony to his will and purpose, and, amidst the greatest revolutions in outward affairs, unerringly interpreting his providence in its bearing on the ends of his Kingdom — testimony and prediction finding their fulfillment in the advent, work, and spiritual Kingdom of the New Testament Redeemer." [3] Archaeology shows that the prophets spoke at definite times during the history of Israel. If we reject prophecy, we must also reject archaeology. And that is bad business, for truth respects things as they *are,* not as we *wish* they were.

The most celebrated event in the New Testament is the resurrection of Christ. The resurrection enjoys this place of honor because it verifies Christ's victory over sin and death (Rom. 1:4). Certainly no event since the world began has been so fully proved by the concurrent testimonies of so many people. Therefore, if we entertain a view of history that excludes the resurrection of Christ, we do more than repudiate Biblical history. We repudiate the very *possibility* of history, for other past events have less evidence in their favor.

And once we grant the validity of Christ's resurrection, we grant the procedure by which miracles in general are verified — including the miracle of fulfilled prophecy.

If a critic rejects the claims of Scripture, he at least ought to acquaint himself with the principle on which he acts. We cannot overturn Christianity without overturning the very standards by which general truth and goodness are decided. This spells skepticism. Paley wisely observes that in judging Christianity, the question lies between this religion and none; for if the Christian religion be not credible, no man can meaningfully support the claims of any other. *Since Christianity is consistent with itself and consistent with the things signified, what relevant criterion of truth is left unappeased?*

Collateral Reading

1. Classics in Christian apologetics: Butler, Joseph, *The Analogy of Religion,* Harper & Brothers, 1855; Paley, William, *A View of the Evidences of Christianity,* R. Faulder, London, 1802. When examining these sources, however, due allowance should be made for

the intellectual climate that prevailed in the seventeenth and eighteenth centuries.

2. The most scholarly series in Christian apologetics: The Bampton Lectures in divinity, and especially the volumes from 1780 to 1892. With the appearance of Sanday's work on *Inspiration* in 1893, the Bampton Lectures began to lose their traditional orthodox stamp.

3. A brilliant satire on David Hume's view of miracles and history: Whately, Richard, *Historic Doubts Relative to Napoleon Buonaparte,* James Monroe & Co., 1843.

4. Methods and techniques of archaeology: Crawford, O. G. S., *Archaeology in the Field,* Phoenix House, London, 1953; Kenyon, Kathleen M., *Beginning in Archaeology,* Phoenix House, London, 1953. Archaeology and the Bible: Albright, William Foxwell, *The Archaeology of Palestine and the Bible,* Fleming H. Revell Company, 1932; *From the Stone Age to Christianity,* The Johns Hopkins Press, 1957, and *Archaeology and the Religion of Israel,* The Johns Hopkins Press, 1942; Keller, Werner, *The Bible as History,* Hodder & Stoughton, London, 1956; Wright, G. Ernest, *Biblical Archaeology,* The Westminster Press, 1957.

VII.

Difficulties

To SAY that orthodoxy is true does not mean that it has no difficulties. Orthodoxy *has* difficulties, and the apologist does not try to conceal them. To affect omniscience is cultic.

Plato set an example of right procedure. First he defended the world of Ideas; then he reviewed the difficulties. He did not fear the difficulties because he believed that the substance of his philosophy was true. No other system could answer the question, How is knowledge possible?

In a similar way, orthodoxy does not fear the difficulties because it believes that the substance of Christianity is true. Christianity is consistent with itself and consistent with the things signified. No other system can answer the question, How can a sinner be just before God?

If a person withholds belief until all difficulties are resolved, he will go to his grave in unbelief, for difficulties are only a sign that we are men and not God. Plato was confined to a cave, while the Christian sees in a mirror dimly. " For our knowledge is imperfect . . . " (I Cor. 13:9.) To confuse a system with its difficulties betrays a want of education.

1. *The Conflict Between Science and Scripture*
Apologists never weary of trying to devise a perfect harmony between science and Scripture, but their efforts are never crowned with success. There are at least three reasons for this. *First,* Scripture

speaks of *ultimate* causes, while science speaks of *proximate* causes. The Bible says that the Lord rained brimstone and fire on Sodom and Gomorrah (Gen. 19:24). But this is not a scientific explanation, and a scientist would be impatient with anyone who said that it was. *Secondly,* Scripture uses optical language when viewing nature. Untrained observers judge appearances; they say, " The sun is setting in the west." The judgment is true, but not as science. *Thirdly,* Scripture speaks of Providence and freedom as well as uniformity. Nature is regular, but it is regular because God decrees it to be regular. Science, on the other hand, speaks only of uniformity.

Theology is beyond its tether when it repudiates uniformity in the name of Providence and freedom, and science is beyond its tether when it repudiates Providence and freedom in the name of uniformity. Legitimate zones of inquiry must be allowed. Calvin suggests a rather happy compromise in his notes on creation: "For, to my mind, this is a certain principle, that nothing is here treated of but the visible form of the world. He who would learn astronomy, and other recondite arts, let him go elsewhere. . . . For Moses here addresses himself to our senses, that the knowledge of the gifts of God which we enjoy may not glide away. . . . By this method . . . the dishonesty of those men is sufficiently rebuked, who censure Moses for not speaking with greater exactness. For as it became a theologian, he had respect to *us* rather than to the stars. . . . Moses wrote in a popular style things which, without instruction, all ordinary persons, endued with common sense, are able to understand; but astronomers investigate with great labor whatever the sagacity of the human mind can comprehend. Nevertheless, this study is not to be reprobated, nor this science to be condemned, because some frantic persons are wont boldly to reject whatever is unknown to them. For astronomy is not only pleasant, but also very useful to be known." [1]

The pretense of theology is often chided; the pretense of science, seldom. For example, it is sometimes said that " science has disproved the possibility of miracles." This is a fatuous boast. Whether miracles have occurred is a matter of *history,* not science. The limits of nature are decided by what has actually happened.

2. *Biological Evolution*

Orthodoxy does not deny that nature is progressively changing, and what is this but evolution? "It may be, I at least am not concerned to deny it, that, within limits which science must define for us, there has been organic evolution — genetic derivation of one order or species of living beings from another. The convergence of many lines of evidence has satisfied the great majority of scientific men at the present day that it is so." [2] The fossil history of the horse rests on rather firmly established data.

Orthodoxy, of course, has little patience with extravagant philosophical reconstructions patterned along the lines of evolution. Scientific evidence is one thing; speculation is another.

Nor is orthodoxy particularly disturbed by the evolution of plants and animals. "And God said, 'Let the earth put forth vegetation.'" (Gen. 1:11.) "And God said, 'Let the earth bring forth living creatures according to their kinds.'" (V. 24.) This language in no way precludes the possibility that present species may have emerged from created latencies. "The physical as such, with its manifold gradations of life and being, its history and developments, its laws of attraction and repulsion, modes of operation, existing forms and possible transformations — all this is either unnoticed in Scripture, or indicated only in its rougher outlines. Even the vexed question respecting the origin and distinctions of species in the animal creation is but partially involved here; for . . . nothing is said as to the number of kinds, or the centers, one or more, in which they respectively originated, how far the several kinds should remain stereotyped, or how far they might be capable, through human art or climatic influences, of departing from the original type, and in process of time developing into varieties and making indefinite approaches one to another." [3]

Evidence for the biological evolution of man, however, cannot be handled with quite this ease. Although man is said to come from the dust, Scripture assigns his distinctive qualities to a divine act of condescension, not to created latencies. There is, as it were, a solemn pause in the creative process: "Then God said, 'Let us make man in our own image, after our likeness.'" (V. 26.) "It is important to notice in what precisely the assertion of this distinctiveness lies. It does not lie in the simple expression, ' Man became a living soul,' for the same words are used in ch. i. 20, 24, 30, to denote purely animal life. Animal, as well as man, is ' living soul.' Neither does it altogether lie in the expression ' breath of lives.'. . . . The true uniqueness in man's formation . . . is expressed by the act of the divine inbreathing, answering somewhat to the *bara* of the previous account. This is an act peculiar to the creation of man; no similar statement is made about the animals. The breath of Jehovah imparts to man the life which is his own, and awakens him to conscious possession of it." [4]

While orthodoxy does not think that the evidence for human evolution is compelling, the evidence *is* sufficient to give pause. The verdict of paleontology cannot be dismissed by pious ridicule. Vital faith builds on general faith, and general faith is a resting of the mind in the sufficiency of the evidences.

When orthodoxy takes inventory of its knowledge, it admits that it does not know *how* God formed man from the dust of the ground. The Genesis account implies an act of immediate creation, but the same account also implies that God made the world in six literal days; and since orthodoxy has given up the literal-day theory out of respect for geology, it would certainly forfeit no principle if it gave up the immediate-creation theory out of respect for paleontology. The two seem to be quite parallel. Moreover, we must be very careful not to prejudice the counsels of God. If God was pleased to breathe his image into a creature that had previously come from the dust, so be it. Scripture only requires us to say that the physical antecedent of man was not denoted *man* until God performed the miraculous act of divine inbreathing. Thus, if science traces man's biological ancestry to dust, Scripture traces his spiritual ancestry to God: ". . . the son of Enos, the son of Seth, the son of Adam, the son of God " (Luke 3:38).

3. *The Unity of the Human Race*

Paleontology denies that the human race is united by a single genetic line. This presents a peculiar difficulty to orthodoxy because of the express manner in which the book of Romans comprehends the entire human race under Adam, the first federal head. Since this teaching falls within the center of a systematic, didactic passage, it cannot be voided without voiding the apostles' right to deliver doctrine on divine authority.

Orthodoxy can do little more than postulate a pre-Adamic race which is structurally similar to Homo sapiens, but which is earlier in time and inferior in endowment. "There is no a priori reason why the creative plan should not have embraced beings showing much nearer approximations to man in structure, and even in a species of intelligence, than have yet been discovered." [5] The postulation has merit, but not much. When prehistoric races give evidence of artifacts and the use of fire, how can they be excluded from the Adamic race? Regardless of how distant a savage may be from the norm of civilization, a missionary addresses him as a partner in the human race.

4. *The Antiquity of the Human Race*

The pre-Abrahamic sections of Scripture form a cluster of difficulties. For example, the story of Babel teaches that all men once lived in a restricted geographical area. But as to when this took place, or how the races diffused throughout the world, no hint is given.

Again, the prima-facie meaning of the Flood is that the entire earth was submerged. Otherwise, how were the mountains covered? But geological evidence fails to verify a universal flood. Orthodoxy has no decisive resolution to offer.

An even greater difficulty grows out of the genealogies in Gen., chs. 5 and 11. It seems that the age of each parent is cited whenever a new generation begins. "When Seth had lived a hundred and five years, he became the father of Enosh. . . . When Enosh had lived ninety years, he became the father of Kenan." (Ch. 5:6, 9.) On the strength of this evidence Archbishop Ussher contended that the creation of man took place in 4004 B.C. This date still appears in some editions of the Bible.

Paleontology has demolished the Ussher chronology. Even a conservative estimate says that man has been on earth from one to two

hundred thousand years. Much of the speculation has been elimi-
nated by new measuring techniques.

The best answer to this difficulty has been given by B. B. Warfield.
Leaning heavily on the pioneer work of William Henry Green,
Warfield developed what orthodoxy calls the "gap theory." The
genealogies of Genesis, says Warfield, "must be esteemed trustworthy for the purposes for which they are recorded; but they cannot safely be pressed into use for other purposes for which they
were not intended, and for which they are not adapted. In particular, it is clear that the genealogical purposes for which the genealogies were given, did not require a complete record of all the generations through which the descent of the persons to whom they are
assigned runs; but only an adequate indication of the particular line
through which the descent in question comes. Accordingly it is
found on examination that the genealogies of Scripture are freely
compressed for all sorts of purposes; and that it can seldom be con-
fidently affirmed that they contain a complete record of the whole
series of generations, while it is often obvious that a very large number are omitted. There is no reason inherent in the nature of the
Scriptural genealogies why a genealogy of ten recorded links, as each
of those in Genesis v. and xi. is, may not represent an actual descent
of a hundred or a thousand or ten thousand links. The point established by the table is not that these are all the links which intervened
between the beginning and the closing names, but that this is the
line of descent through which one traces back to or down to the
other." [6]

The "gap theory" is attractive because there *are* gaps in the genealogies. But no conclusive proof is given that the gaps are sufficiently
numerous or wide to accommodate the vast antiquity of man.

5. *Higher Criticism*

Orthodoxy welcomes any investigation that throws light on the
literary and historical background of the Bible. "If the Scriptures
have God as their author, it surely concerns us all the more on that
account, to have them submitted to the most searching critical scrutiny." [7] Again, "I do not believe . . . that any really devout stu-

dent of the Bible desires to tie up honest inquiry on any question of author, origin, date, or mode of composition of the Biblical books, which does not involve clear contradiction of the Bible's own testimony on these subjects. By all means, if any traditional opinion can be shown by valid reasoning on sound data to be in error on such points, let it be corrected." [8]

After saying this, however, orthodoxy faces no small difficulty deciding where legitimate criticism begins and ends. Some exegetes say that Ecclesiastes was written by Solomon; others, that an unknown author spoke in the name of the king's son, in an effort to dignify his narrative. Some say that Isaiah had one author; others, that parts of the book were written by a school of prophets. And so it goes. A measure of Christian charity is needed at this point, though orthodoxy is rarely willing to give it.

An outsider may wonder how orthodoxy can repudiate destructive higher criticism and still claim to be honest before the facts. The mystery is easily cleared up. " Destructive criticism is great and vigorous; it is learned and acute; it may possibly have just cause for its open contempt for the learning, the acuteness, the argumentative force and literary ability of the defenders of the trustworthiness of the Bible. But it does not reckon sufficiently with one fact. It has the Bible itself against it, and the Bible is always with us. When this criticism has been forgotten, the Bible will still be read by men, and will still convey to men its own views of the course of the history by which the true religion has been given by God to man." [9]

6. The Problem of Textual Harmony

Not all of orthodoxy's difficulties trace to friction between Scripture, science, and destructive criticism. There are problems inherent in the Biblical text itself. And we do not refer to passages where the Hebrew or Greek is obscure; we refer to passages that are ostensibly clear. For example, Jude says, " It was of these also that Enoch in the seventh generation from Adam prophesied, saying ' Behold, the Lord came with his holy myriads.' " (Jude 14.) Jude credits Enoch, the seventh from Adam, while external evidence credits the apocryphal Book of Enoch. Of course, orthodoxy can always say that

Jude knew by inspiration that the seventh from Adam spoke the words that now appear in the Book of Enoch; but the explanation sounds suspiciously affected.

Orthodoxy has never arranged a perfect harmony of the Gospels. For example, Mark says that a staff *should* be taken, Matthew that a staff should *not* be taken. " He charged them to take nothing for their journey except a staff." (Mark 6:8.) " Take no gold, nor silver, nor copper in your belts, no bag for your journey, nor two tunics, nor sandals, nor a staff." (Matt. 10:9–10.) About all orthodoxy can say is that data or circumstances are kept back which, if known, would resolve the inconsistency. It should not be supposed, however, that the Synoptics are replete with difficulties. General harmony has been established.

Even the claims of Romans and Galatians can be embarrassed by scattered verses in the Bible. For example, Romans says that *faith* is the instrumental cause of justification. Yet, when Ananias advises Paul, he uses language that suggests that *baptism* is the instrumental cause: " And now why do you wait? Rise and be baptized, and wash away your sins, calling on his name " (Acts 22:16). Peter uses similar language: " Baptism, which corresponds to this [Noah's ark], now saves you, not as a removal of dirt from the body but as an appeal to God for a clear conscience " (I Peter 3:21).

It is extremely difficult, if not impossible, to coax all the Biblical data into neat harmony. But this want of precision in no way affects the substance of the Biblical system. The rules of hermeneutics see to that. Theology is drawn from those portions of Scripture which have theology in view; and theology is the norm by which everything else in Scripture is understood. Whenever a passage conflicts with the teaching of Romans and Galatians, either the mind has failed to grasp its meaning, or the passage falls under the concept of progressive revelation.

7. *The Nature of Inspiration*

Although orthodoxy stoutly defends the doctrine of inspiration, it has never devised an official view of inspiration. At least two schools of thought vie for primacy. The first is known as the Princeton

Theology, while the second received its classical expression in Great Britain.

The Princeton Theology was brought to fruition by the two giants of Presbyterianism, Charles Hodge and B. B. Warfield. Their labor is possibly the finest theological and apologetical thrust in the history of American orthodoxy. Few men have equaled — certainly none has surpassed — the acuteness of these scholars.

The Princeton Theology contends that inspiration communicates truth on divine authority. The Scriptural expression " it is written " means " God says it." And whatever God says, is true because he says it. "*Inspiration is that extraordinary, supernatural influence (or, passively, the result of it) exerted by the Holy Ghost on the writers of our Sacred Books, by which their words were rendered also the words of God, and, therefore, perfectly infallible.*" [10]

The texts that teach plenary inspiration are legion. Their force, says Warfield, cannot be dodged. " The effort to explain away the Bible's witness to its plenary inspiration reminds one of a man standing safely in his laboratory and elaborately expounding . . . how every stone in an avalanche has a defined pathway and may easily be dodged by one of some presence of mind. We may fancy such an elaborate trifler's triumph as he would analyze the avalanche into its constituent stones, and demonstrate of stone after stone that its pathway is definite, limited, and may easily be avoided. But avalanches, unfortunately, do not come upon us, stone by stone, one at a time, courteously leaving us opportunity to withdraw from the pathway of each in turn: but all at once, in a roaring mass of destruction. Just so we may explain away a text or two which teach plenary inspiration . . . but these texts of ours, again, unfortunately, do not come upon us in this artificial isolation; neither are they few in number. There are scores, hundreds, of them: and they come bursting upon us in one solid mass." [11]

The second school of thought was headed by the gifted English polemicist, James Orr. The communication of *life,* not knowledge, is the goal of inspiration. " In the last resort, the proof of the inspiration of the Bible . . . is to be found in the life-giving effects which that message has produced, wherever its word of truth has gone.

This is the truth in the argument for inspiration based on the witness of the Holy Spirit. The Bible has the qualities claimed for it as
an inspired book. . . . It leads to God and to Christ; it gives light
on the deepest problems of life, death, and eternity; it discovers the
way of deliverance from sin; it makes men new creatures; it furnishes the man of God completely for every good work." [12] Orr is
an outspoken critic of the Princeton Theology. " The older method
was to prove first the inspiration . . . then through that establish
the revelation. This view still finds an echo in the note sometimes
heard — ' If the inspiration of the Bible (commonly some *theory* of
inspiration) be given up, what have we left to hold by? ' It is urged,
e.g., that unless we can demonstrate what is called the ' inerrancy '
of the Biblical record, down even to its minutest details, the whole
edifice of belief in revealed religion falls to the ground. This, on the
face of it, is a most suicidal position for any defender of revelation
to take up. It is certainly a much easier matter to prove the reality of
a divine revelation in the history of Israel, or in Christ, than it is
to prove the inerrant inspiration of every part of the record through
which that revelation has come to us." [13]

Two things can be said about this cleavage in orthodoxy: *first,*
each school of thought tries to be honest with what Scripture teaches;
secondly, each school builds its case on what it believes is the chief
emphasis in Scripture. Apparently some passages connect inspiration with truth on divine authority, while others connect it with
power to communicate life in Christ. The Princeton Theology
draws on the first body of verses: " If we are to occupy the attitude
toward Scripture which Christ occupied, the simple ' It is written! '
must have the same authority to us in matters of doctrinal truth, of
practical duty, of historical fact and of verbal form that it had to
him; and to us as truly as to him, the Scriptures must be incapable
of being broken." [14] The English school draws on the verses that link
inspiration with power to communicate life in Christ: " Inspiration,
Paul says, confers on Scripture the properties of being ' profitable
for teaching, for reproof, for correction, for instruction which is in
righteousness ' — of being able ' to make wise unto salvation through
faith which is in Christ Jesus.' Of similar nature are the qualities

ascribed in the psalms to the law of God — 'restoring the soul,' 'making wise the simple,' 'rejoicing the heart,' 'enlightening the eyes,' etc." [15]

The cleavage in orthodoxy is partly a reflection of the Biblical text itself. The passages on inspiration are apparently too rich and variegated to be comprehended under the limitations of any single theory.

It should be observed, however, that both schools of orthodoxy agree that God made a covenant with Abraham, and that Jesus Christ is the blessing of this covenant. Orthodoxy does not consider inspiration an end in itself. Whether *truth* or *power* is stressed, the Bible illuminates our pathway to Jesus Christ.

8. Does Inspiration Correct the Sources?

In due time the Princeton Theology was attacked by divines within the Presbyterian Church itself. And spearheading this attack was the incisive Old Testament critic, Henry Preserved Smith. This protracted exchange of convictions was possibly the last great dialogue on inspiration in America.

Smith lost no time in challenging Warfield's central thesis, namely, that the Scriptural expression " it is written " means " God says it." " Now, turning to the First Epistle to the Corinthians (iii, 19), we read: ' *For it is written,* He that taketh the wise in their craftiness.' The quotation from the Old Testament is found in Job v, 13, in a speech of Eliphaz the Temanite. But the speeches of Eliphaz are not accepted by the most stringent inerrancist as 'infallible in all their utterances.'" [16] It should be said that Smith was entirely correct in this contention, for orthodoxy freely admitted that the speeches of Eliphaz are not divinely inspired. " Special stress is laid in this connection, on the phenomena of The Book of Job, where one man teaches one doctrine, and another another. But Job's friends were not inspired. All our doctrine demands, is that the writer of that book was inspired to give a true account, first of what the men said, and then of what God said." [17] But when orthodoxy made this admission, it saddled itself with a very troublesome expedient. Whether orthodoxy realized it or not, it was really saying that inspiration, at times, ensures no more than an infallible account of error. This was such an ironic admission that Smith lost no time pressing it to advantage. " We have the prosecution, then, conceding that the speeches of Eliphaz, as recorded for us by inspiration, are not guaranteed as infallible. Yet one of these speeches is quoted by the very formula which, as the prosecution assert, declares Scripture to be infallible in all its utterances. The inconsistency is apparent. The phrase *it is written* is in one case, at least, not an assertion of infallibility, and of course it can not be made such an assertion anywhere else." [18]

When once Smith had forced the Princeton Theology into the awkward position of admitting that inspiration, at times, ensures no more than an infallible account of error, he ransacked the Old Testament for all sorts of troublesome passages. And the most troublesome were drawn from parallel accounts in the historical books. The following are striking examples.

II Sam. viii:4. And David took from him 1,700 horsemen and 20,000 footmen.	I Chron. xviii:3. And David took from him 1,000 chariots, and 7,000 horsemen, and 20,000 footmen.
x:6. The children of Ammon sent and hired the Syrians of Beth Rehob and the Syrians of Zobah 20,000 footmen, and the King of Maacah with 1,000 men, and the men of Tob, 1,200 men.	xix:6. Hanun and the children of Ammon sent 1,000 talents of silver to hire them chariots and horsemen. So they hired them 32,000 chariots and the King of Maacah and his men.
x:18. David destroyed of the Syrians 700 chariots.	xix:18. David destroyed of the Syrians 7,000 chariots.
xxiv:9. There were in Israel 800,000 valiant men who drew sword, and the men of Judah were 500,000.	xxi:5. There were of all Israel 1,100,000 that drew sword and Judah was 370,000 that drew sword.
xxiv:24. So David bought the threshing floor and the oxen for 50 shekels in silver.	xxi:25. So David gave to Ornan for the place 600 shekels of gold by weight.

I Kings, iv:26. And Solomon had 40,000 stalls for horses.	II Chron. ix:25. And Solomon had 4,000 stalls for horses and chariots.
vi:2. The height [of the house] 30 cubits.	iii:4. The height [of the porch] 120 cubits.
vii:26. It [the brazen sea] held 2,000 baths.	iv:5. It received and held 3,000 baths.

"Now, it will be said at once that these are all discrepancies in numbers which are very liable to corruption, and that, therefore, these are all cases of error in transmission. But I ask you to notice that these are all but one, cases in which the larger number is in the text of the Chronicler. Where the age of a king or the length of his reign is concerned I have not taken account of the difference. But in matters of statistics it is curious that the errors should be nearly all one way. Remembering that the Chronicler was much farther away in time from the events narrated, we find it natural that he should have an exaggerated idea of the resources of his country in the days of her glory. In the case of David's purchase of the field of Ornan, he finds the price a niggardly one for a prince to pay. He, therefore, does not hesitate (supposing that a mistake has been made) to put in a larger sum." [19]

Warfield found these problems disturbing but not distressing. And behind his complacency was the following theological conviction: Regardless how plausible a theory of inspiration may be, or how successful it is in resolving difficulties, it does not accord with truth, and must be rejected, if it conflicts with the testimony of Christ and the apostles. "If we accept the full authority of Christ and his apostles in all things, we must accept the infallible Bible at their hands." [20] Either the apostles are bearers of doctrine or they are not. If they are, the church is bound by their teaching on inspiration; and if they are not, Christian theology forfeits its objectivity. "The real problem brought before the churches by the present debate ought now to be sufficiently plain. In its deepest essence it is whether we can still trust the Bible as a guide in doctrine, as a teacher of truth. It is not simply whether we can explain away the Biblical doctrine of inspiration so as to allow us to take a different view from what has been common of the structure and characteristics of the Bible. Nor, on the other hand, is it simply whether we may easily explain the facts, established as facts, embedded in Scripture, consistently with the teaching of Scripture as to the nature, extent, and effects of inspiration. It is specifically whether the results proclaimed by a special school of Biblical criticism — which are of such a character, as is now admitted by all, as to necessitate, if adopted, a new view of the Bible and of its inspiration — rest on a basis of evidence strong enough to meet and overcome the weight of evidence, whatever that may be in kind and amount, which goes to show that the Bible writers are trustworthy as teachers of doctrine. If we answer this question in the affirmative, then no doubt we shall have not only a new view of the Bible and of its inspiration but also a whole new theology, because we must seek a new basis for doctrine. But if we answer it in the negative, we may possess our souls in patience and be assured that the Scriptures are as trustworthy witnesses to truth when they declare a doctrine of inspiration as when they declare a doctrine of incarnation or of redemption, even though in the one case as in the other, difficulties may remain, the full explanation of which is not yet clear to us. The real question, in a word, is not a new question but the perennial old question, whether the basis of our doctrine is to be what the Bible teaches, or what men teach. And this is a question which is to be settled on the old method, viz., on our estimate of the weight and value of the evidence which places the Bible in our hands as a teacher of doctrine." [21]

Warfield was content to rest his case at this point. Since Smith had accommodated the doctrine of inspiration to the inductive difficulties, he forfeited the principle by which *any* Christian doctrine is established. The result, of necessity, was a loss of normative Christianity. "It is everywhere apparent that when he [Smith] denies that the Scriptures are free from error, he means as much as those words can be made to include, not as little as possible: and that his object is not to leave the way open enough not to be disturbed by

' specks in the marble of the Parthenon ' or slight blemishes in accuracy of statement; but to leave it open wide enough to reject the authority of this or the other whole section of Bible history or this or the other whole sphere of Bible declaration." [22]

But Warfield became so enamored of the norm by which doctrine is established, that he took a rather easy attitude toward the inductive difficulties. Instead of answering the particular problems raised by Smith, he preferred to debate the question on the level of doctrine. " The difference between him [Smith] and the church in this matter does not lie where he fancies it does. It lies here: he has more confidence in his own historical judgments than in Scriptural statements, and prefers to harmonize the Scriptural statements with his opinions. The church has more confidence in the Scriptural statements than in his historical opinions, and prefers that he shall harmonize his opinions with the Scriptural statements. Dr. Smith says it cannot be done. Well, then, the issue is sharply drawn. And in the last analysis it is simply this: Infallible Scripture *versus* Infallible Science." [23] This is a very forthright position to take, but it hardly does justice to the inductive difficulties in the text.

The ecclesiastical struggle between Smith and the Princeton divines provoked a new dialogue within orthodoxy itself. And once again the burden of leadership fell on James Orr. In the judgment of Orr, it is neither fair nor prudent to fly in the face of inductive difficulties. If orthodoxy is to command the respect of scholarship, it must become more artistic and imaginative when it relates the doctrine of inspiration to wider claims of Scripture.

Orr, let us remember, links inspiration with the dynamic work of uniting a sinner with Jesus Christ. Sometimes this work assumes the form of poetry (Psalms), sometimes history (Kings and Chronicles), and sometimes propositional revelation (Romans and Galatians). Poetry is mediated by religious experience; history (in many cases), by evidence drawn from existing documents; and doctrine, by direct revelation. Each aspect of Scripture is sufficient for its own end. Thus, while the *whole* Bible is inspired, inspiration is pluralistic in substance; and it is pluralistic because in the single work of drawing men to Christ, various kinds of evidence are used. Poetry charms, history informs, and doctrine binds.

James Orr drew on these convictions when he faced the seeming disharmony between the Chronicles and other Old Testament histories. First, he *acknowledged* the problem. He did not sweep it under the rug of theological tradition. He then went on to ask what purpose inspiration served in the Chronicles. And for this second inquiry he turned to the pious and learned Matthew Henry: " As to the difficulties that occur in this and the foregoing genealogies we need not perplex ourselves. I presume Ezra took them as he found them *in the books of the kings of Israel and Judah* (ch. ix.1.), according as they were given in by the several tribes, each observing what method they thought fit. Hence some *a*scend, other *de*scend; some have *numbers* affixed, others *places;* some have historical remarks intermixed, others have not; some are shorter, others longer; some agree with other records, others differ; some, it is likely, were torn, erased, and blotted, others more legible. Those of Dan and Reuben were entirely lost. This holy man wrote as he was moved by the Holy Ghost; but there was no necessity for the making up of the defects, no, nor for the rectifying of the mistakes, of these genealogies by inspiration. It was sufficient that he copied them out as they came to his hand, or so much of them as was requisite to the present purpose, which was the directing of the returned captives to settle as nearly as they could with those of their own family, and in the places of their former residence. We may suppose that many things in these genealogies which to us seem intricate, abrupt, and perplexed, were plain and easy to them then (who knew how to fill up the deficiencies) and abundantly answered the intention of the publishing of them." [24] Since the Chronicles were aimed at acquainting the returning captives with their heritage, this purpose was accomplished by the publication of data drawn from existing documents. The Holy Spirit used the documents just as they were.

James Orr has his own incisive way of putting the matter: " It is not uncommon to hear inspiration spoken of as if it rendered the subject of it superior to ordinary sources of information, or at least was at hand to supply supernaturally all gaps or deficiencies in that information. The records of the Bible have only to be studied as they lie before us to show that this is an entire mistake. . . . In *historical* matters it is evident that inspiration is dependent for its knowledge of facts on the ordinary channels of information — on older documents, on oral tradition, on public registers, on genealogical lists, etc. No sober-minded defender of inspiration would now think of denying this proposition. One has only to look into the Biblical books to discover the abundant proof of it. The claim made is that the sources of information are *good,* trustworthy, not that inspiration lifts the writer above the need of dependence on them. . . . Thus, for the history of David, reference is made to three works — the Book of Samuel the Seer, the Book of Nathan the Prophet, the Book of Gad the Seer. For numerous reigns extracts are given from ' the Book of the Chronicles of the Kings of Israel ' (or ' of the Kings of Judah ' or ' of the Kings of Israel and Judah '). . . . Where sources of information fail, or where, as may sometimes happen, there are lacunae, or blots, or misreadings of names, or errors of transcription, such as are incidental to the transmission of all MSS., it is not to be supposed that supernatural information is granted to supply the lack. Where this is frankly acknowledged, inspiration is cleared from a great many of the difficulties which misapprehension has attached to it." [25]

The Princeton Theology did not deny that existing documents were used in the historical sections of the Bible. It merely assumed that if inspiration guaranteed anything at all, it guaranteed an infallible text. " The natural knowledge [used by the Biblical historians] came from all sources, as traditions, documents, testimonies, personal observations, and recollections . . . yet all were alike under the general direction of God's providence. The supernatural knowledge became confluent with the natural in a manner which violated no law of reason or of freedom. And throughout the whole of his work the Holy Spirit was present, causing his energies to flow into the spontaneous exercises of the writer's faculties, elevating and directing where need be, and everywhere securing the errorless expression in language of the thought designed by God. This last element we call inspiration." [26]

It should not be supposed, however, that James Orr dominated the English scene. Other apologists took a position that was not materially different from the Princeton Theology. James Bannerman is a typical representative: " If Scripture to an unknown and indefinite extent is not historically true, there is no Christian apologist that will waste time in the endeavor to prove that it is supernaturally true." [27]

Orr would probably answer Bannerman in the following way: Since the purpose of inspiration is to communicate life in Christ, this purpose is reached whether or not the Holy Spirit corrected the documents from which the Chronicler drew his information. God does all things perfectly, but the standard of this perfection is the will of God, not the will of man. And one instrument under the will of God is the inspired Chronicler — inspired, that is, to make us wise unto salvation, and not to supply us with an infallible review of Semitic history.

The dialogue between Orr and the Princeton Theology was never successfully terminated. The problem of inspiration is *still* a problem. " The words of Job and of Job's friends, and to some extent of Elihu, require to be tested and corroborated by the undoubted utterances of the Lord and his prophets elsewhere, before we can affirm them as correct statements of divine truth. The same rule applies to all speeches of uninspired persons recorded in Scripture. Saint Stephen's speech, being the speech of an inspired person, delivered under cover of a special promise, may be defended as itself inspired. *But the Scripture in Acts vii. is not St. Stephen's speech, but St. Luke's record of what Stephen said.* And, therefore, a mistake in the speech (if there were one, which has never been proved) could not be alleged as a mistake in Holy Scripture. . . . For if St. Stephen did err, St. Luke, as a faithful reporter, was bound to record his error when he reported the speech. Obviously the question how far this principle is to be applied requires some thought and consideration. Does it extend to the sentiments expressed in the song of Deborah and Barak, for example? The Scripture in Judges v. is the record of what they sang. If the blessed Jael, the Scripture must record the blessing. But does the Scripture, by recording what was spoken, endorse all that was said? . . . This is a matter on which a man should be fully persuaded before he presumes to dogmatize. . . . When, therefore, we affirm that all Scripture is to be taken as divine law, we mean that it has the force of law, so far, and in such a sense, as each particular writing is capable of legal force. The history in Scripture to a great extent is law in the form of precedent. It is the record of cases in which the law has been correctly applied — an infallible set of precedents. The poetry of Scripture is law so far as poetry can have that force. Where it expresses the divine mind, it is absolute. Where it expresses the human feelings, confessions, and aspirations of God's people, it unveils the secret history of his children, and supplies us with many a precedent for our instruction, edification, and comfort. But the question, how far The Psalms (for instance) can be taken as expressions of the divine mind in all cases, is one that deserves more attention than it has received. When Jeremiah (xx.14) says, ' Cursed be the day wherein I was born '; and ' Cursed be the man who brought tidings to my father,' &c., we do not attach much greater weight to this outburst than to that of Job in the second week of his misery (Job iii.3, &c.). But what are we to say to the recorded language of the captives by the waters of Babylon, ' Happy shall he be that taketh and dasheth thy little ones against the stones ' (Psa. cxxxvii. end) ? Does the mere fact that these words occur in the Psalter make the *human* feeling which stimulated them itself faultless and divine? " [28]

Contemporary orthodoxy does very little to sustain the classical dialogue on inspiration. The fountain of new ideas has apparently run dry, for what was once a live issue in the church has now ossified into a theological tradition. As a result a heavy pall of fear hangs over the academic community. When a gifted professor tries to interact with the critical difficulties in the text, he is charged with disaffection, if not outright heresy. Orthodoxy forgets one important verdict of history: namely, that when truth is presented in a poor light, tomorrow's leaders may embrace error on the single reason that it is more persuasively defended.

9. *Conclusion*

Three terminal observations must be made. *First,* classical orthodoxy rests its doctrine of inspiration on the testimony of Christ and the apostles. A fair and honest effort is then made to harmonize this testimony with the inductive difficulties in the text. *But in no case is the doctrine of inspiration accommodated to the difficulties.* If orthodoxy were to tolerate such accommodation, it would forfeit the principle by which *any* Christian doctrine is established. This would banish theology to the wastelands of subjectivity.

Secondly, even if it could be shown that the Chronicles are not entirely compatible with other Old Testament histories, the doctrine of Biblical inerrancy would *not* be demolished. Orthodoxy would simply shift its conception of the thing signified. Just as the inspired author of Job gives an infallible account of what Eliphaz said, so the inspired author of Chronicles gives an infallible account of what was said in the public registers and genealogical lists. At first blush this may seem like a very desperate expedient, but it actually implies no more than a strained use of procedures already at work in orthodoxy. If Hodge and Warfield had honored this as a possibility, they might have avoided their lofty disregard for the inductive difficulties. And if Orr had done likewise, he might have avoided his perilous admission of historical errors in Scripture.

Orthodoxy could profitably spend more time examining the relation between *assertion* and the *thing signified*. For example, on what standard was Semitic history written? Does poetry communicate feeling or truth? Is recorded religious experience normative for believers in another economy? Orthodoxy works itself into excessive difficulties by artlessly defining the relation between assertion and the thing signified. Crass literalism is hardly a worthy answer to irresponsible allegorizing.

Thirdly, orthodoxy may never officially decide whether the Holy Spirit corrected the documents from which the Chronicler drew his information. But this irresolution does not affect the theology of the church, for Paul received his theology directly from Jesus Christ (Gal. 1:11-12). He did *not* draw on existing documents. And theology is the norm by which a Christian understands everything else in Scripture — including the Chronicles of Israel which drew on sources which may or may not have been corrected by the Holy Spirit. Orthodoxy's intramural debate on inspiration in no way disturbs the truth of the gospel, and to think that it does is cultic.

Collateral Reading

1. Miracles and the limits of science: Clark, Gordon H., "Miracles, History, and Natural Law," in *The Evangelical Quarterly*, Vol. 12 (1940), pp. 23–34. The struggle between science and theology: Jellema, Dirk, "Genesis and Science in John Calvin," in *The Reformed Journal*, Vol. VI, No. 3 (March, 1956), pp. 17–19; White, Andrew Dickson, *A History of the Warfare of Science with Theology in Christendom*, 2 vols., D. Appleton & Company, 1922.

2. The problem of human antiquity: Green, William Henry, "Primeval Chronology," in *Bibliotheca Sacra*, Vol. XLVII (1890), pp. 285–303; Orr, James, *God's Image in Man*, pp. 139–193, Wm. B. Eerdmans Publishing Company, 1948; Urquhart, John, *How Old Is Man?* James Nisbet & Co., Ltd., London, 1904; Warfield, B. B., "On the Antiquity and Unity of the Human Race," in *Biblical and Theological Studies*, pp. 238–261, The Presbyterian and Reformed Publishing Company, 1952.

3. Difficulties in the Bible: Haley, John W., *An Examination of the Alleged Discrepancies of the Bible*, B. C. Goodpasture, Nashville, Tenn., 1951; Lee, William, *The Inspiration of Holy Scripture*, 3d edition, pp. 369–424, Hodges, Smith & Company, Dublin, 1864. The Lutheran dialogue on inspiration: Preus, Robert, *The Inspiration of Scripture*, Oliver & Boyd, Ltd., Edinburgh, 1955.

4. The validity of Christ's resurrection: Niebuhr, Richard R., *Resurrection and Historical Reason*, Charles Scribner's Sons, 1957.

5. The problem of chronology in the Kingdoms of Israel and Judah: Thiele, Edwin R., *The Mysterious Numbers of the Hebrew Kings*, The University of Chicago Press, 1951.

VIII.

Perils

ORTHODOXY is plagued by perils as well as difficulties, and the perils are even more disturbing than the difficulties. When orthodoxy slights its difficulties, it elicits criticism; but when it slights its perils, it elicits scorn. The perils are of two sorts — general and specific. The general perils include ideological thinking, a highly censorious spirit, and a curious tendency to separate from the life of the church. The specific peril is the ease with which orthodoxy converts to fundamentalism. *Fundamentalism is orthodoxy gone cultic.*

1. *Fundamentalism*

When we speak of fundamentalism, however, we must distinguish between the movement and the mentality. The fundamentalist movement was organized shortly after the turn of the twentieth century. When the tidal wave of German higher criticism engulfed the church, a large company of orthodox scholars rose to the occasion. They sought to prove that modernism and Biblical Christianity were incompatible. In this way the fundamentalist movement preserved the faith once for all delivered to the saints. Its " rugged bursts of individualism " were among the finest fruits of the Reformation.

But the fundamentalist movement made at least one capital mistake, and this is why it converted from a movement to a mentality. Unlike the Continental Reformers and the English Dissenters, the fundamentalists failed to connect their convictions with the classical creeds of the church. Therefore, when modernism collapsed, the fundamentalist movement became an army without a cause. Nothing was left but the mentality of fundamentalism, and this mentality is orthodoxy's gravest peril.

The mentality of fundamentalism is dominated by ideological thinking. Ideological thinking is rigid, intolerant, and doctrinaire; it sees principles everywhere, and all principles come in clear tones of black and white; it exempts itself from the limits that original sin places on history; it wages holy wars without acknowledging the elements of pride and personal interest that prompt the call to battle; it creates new evils while trying to correct old ones.

The fundamentalists' crusade against the Revised Standard Version illustrates the point. The fury did not stem from a scholarly conviction that the version offends Hebrew and Greek idioms, for ideological thinking operates on far simpler criteria. *First,* there were modernists on the translation committee, and modernists corrupt whatever they touch. It does not occur to fundamentalism that translation requires only personal honesty and competent scholarship. *Secondly,* the Revised Standard Version's copyright is held by the Division of Christian Education of the National Council of the Churches of Christ. If a fundamentalist used the new version, he might give aid and comfort to the National Council; and that, on his principles, would be sin. By the same token, of course, a fundamentalist could not even buy groceries from a modernist. But ideological thinking is never celebrated for its consistency.

2. *J. Gresham Machen*

The mentality of fundamentalism sometimes crops up where one would least expect it; and there is no better illustration of this than the inimitable New Testament scholar, J. Gresham Machen. Machen was an outspoken critic of the fundamentalist movement. He argued with great force that Christianity is a *system,* not a list of fundamentals. The fundamentals include the virgin birth, Christ's deity and miracles, the atonement, the resurrection, and the inspiration of the Bible. But this list does not even take in the specific issues of the Protestant Reformation. Roman Catholicism easily falls within the limits of fundamentalism.

While Machen was a foe of the fundamentalist movement, he was a friend of the fundamentalist mentality, for he took an absolute stand on a relative issue, and the wrong issue at that.

Machen gained prominence through his litigations with the Presbyterian Church U.S.A. He contended that when the church has modernists in its agencies and among its officially supported missionaries, a Christian has no other course than to withdraw support. So Machen promptly set up "The Independent Board for Presbyterian Foreign Missions"; and with equal promptness the General Assembly ordered the Board dissolved. Machen disobeyed the order on the conviction that he could appeal from the General Assembly to the Constitution of the church. But this conviction traced to ideological thinking, for if a federal system is to succeed, supreme judicial power must be vested in one court. This is federalism's answer to the threat of anarchy. Wrong decisions by a court are not irremediable; but until due process of law effects a reversal, a citizen must obey or be prosecuted.

Machen became so fixed on the evil of modernism that he did not see the evil of anarchy. This fixation prompted him to follow a course that eventually offended the older and wiser Presbyterians. These men knew that nothing constructive would be gained by defying the courts of the church. Perhaps the General Assembly had made a mistake; but until the action was reversed by due process of law, obedience was required. No individual Presbyterian can appeal from the General Assembly to the Constitution, and to think that he can is cultic.

Ideological thinking prevented Machen from seeing that the issue under trial was *the nature of the church,* not the doctrinal incompatibility of orthodoxy and modernism. Does the church become apostate when it has modernists in its agencies and among its officially supported missionaries? The older Presbyterians knew enough about Reformed ecclesiology to answer this in the negative. Unfaithful ministers do *not* render the church apostate. "Dreadful are those descriptions in which Isaiah, Jeremiah, Joel, Habakkuk, and others, deplore the disorders of the church of Jerusalem. There was such general and extreme corruption in the people, in the magistrates, and in the priests, that Isaiah does not hesitate to compare Jerusalem to Sodom and Gomorrah. Religion was partly despised, partly corrupted. Their manners were generally disgraced by thefts, robberies, treacheries, murders, and similar crimes. Nevertheless, the prophets on this account neither raised themselves new churches, nor built new altars for the oblation of separate sacrifices; but whatever were the characters of the people, yet because they considered that God had deposited his word among that nation, and instituted the ceremonies in which he was there worshiped, they lifted up pure hands to him even in the congregation of the impious. If they had thought that they contracted any contagion from these services, surely they would have suffered a hundred deaths rather than have permitted themselves to be dragged to them. There was nothing therefore to prevent their departure from them, but the desire of preserving the unity of the church. But if the holy prophets were restrained by a sense of duty from forsaking the church on account of the numerous and enormous crimes which were practiced, not by a few individuals, but almost by the whole nation — it is extreme arrogance in us, if we presume immediately to withdraw from the communion of a church where the conduct of all members is not compatible either with our judgment, or even with the Christian profession." [1]

Machen thought it would be easy to purify the church. All one had to do was to withdraw from modernists; the expedient was as simple as that. " On Thursday, June 11, 1936," said Machen to his loyal remnant, " the hopes of many long years were realized. We became members, at last, of a true Presbyterian church." It was not long, however, before Machen's true church was locked in the convulsions of internal strife. The prophecy of the older Presbyterians was fulfilled. Since Machen had shaken off the sins of modernists, but not the sins of those who were proud they were not modernists, the separatists fondly imagined themselves more perfectly delivered from heresy than the facts justified. This illusion spawned fresh resources of pride and pretense. The criteria of Christian fellowship gradually became more exacting than Scripture, and before long Machen himself was placed under suspicion. He had not taken his reformation far enough: the church was not yet true. This time the issue was not modernism; the issue, ostensibly, was dispensationalism and Christian liberty. And before this quarrel ended, a *second* true church was founded.

Still, no classical effort was made to define the nature of the church. This is how the mentality of fundamentalism operates. Status by negation, not precise theological inquiry, is the first order of business. When there are no modernists from which to withdraw, fundamentalists compensate by withdrawing from one another.

Machen tried to blend the classical view of the covenant with a separatist view of the covenant people. He honored Reformed doctrine, but not the Reformed doctrine of the church. This inconsistency had at least two effects: *first,* it encouraged Machen's disciples to think that the conditions of Christian fellowship could be decided by subjective criteria; *secondly,* it planted the seeds of anarchy. If Reformed theology could not define the nature of the church, how could it define the nature of anything else? The result was a subtle reversion to the age of the Judges: each man did what was right in his own eyes. Rebellion against the courts of the church converted to rebellion against the wisdom of the ages and the counsel of the brethren.

3. *Dispensationalism*

Having drifted from the classical creeds of the church, the separatist is prey to theological novelty. Most of Machen's immediate disciples were shielded from this threat by their orientation in Calvinism, but fundamentalism in general did not fare so well. Dispensationalism filled the vacuum created by the loss of the historic creeds.

Dispensationalism was formulated by one of the nineteenth-century separatist movements, the Plymouth Brethren. Hitherto, all Christians had believed that the church fulfills the prophecies of the Old Testament, and that the future of saved Jews falls within the general life of the church. Dispensationalism overturned this time-tested confession by contending that the church is only an interim period between two Jewish economies, the Old Testament and the millennium.

While dispensationalism sincerely tries to honor the distinctives of Christianity, in practice it often honors the distinctives of Judaism. This is an ironic reversal. " It is strange . . . that the unbelieving Jews should be represented as nearly *right* in their interpretation of the prophecies respecting the Messiah. We know that the whole, or very nearly the whole, of the nation looked for a temporal deliverance — for a Christ who would be a triumphant conqueror, to deliver them out of the hands of their temporal enemies. We know that it was this strong expectation *that led most of them to reject Jesus;* and that they were buoyed up, especially during the last siege, with the hope of a Christ coming to deliver them; and that this character was claimed by several pretenders, who accordingly obtained numerous followers. Now, according to the above scheme, Christ *is* to come as a victorious temporal deliverer of the Jews, and is to fulfill the prophecies just in the sense in which *they* have always understood them. If so, those who rejected Jesus were, on the whole, nearly right in their interpretation of the prophecies, and were only mistaken as to *the time;* which is very much what the Jews hold at this day." [2]

Having withdrawn from the general theological dialogue, the dispensationalist has few active checks against the pretense of ideological pride. As a result, he imagines that the distinctives of dispensationalism are more firmly established than they really are. This illusion prompts him to fight major battles over minor issues. If it comes to it, he is not unwilling to divide the church on whether the rapture occurs before or after the tribulation. This is straight-line cultic conduct, for a cursory examination of Philip Schaff's *Creeds of Christendom* will show that the church has *never* made the details of eschatology a test of Christian fellowship. The dispensationalist is willing to go it alone because he is prompted by the counsels of ideological thinking. He compares Biblical doctrines to a line of standing dominoes: topple any one domino and the entire line falls. On such a scheme the time of the rapture is as crucial to faith as the substitutionary atonement, for any one doctrine analytically includes all other doctrines. This argument, of course, is a tissue of fallacies. It violates the most elementary canons of Biblical hermeneutics.

When separatists flee from the tyranny of the church, they end up with a new tyranny all their own; for there is always a demagogue on hand to decide who is virtuous and who is not. His strategies are pathetically familiar: "Things are in terrible shape; errorists are everywhere. The true faith is being threatened; my own life is in danger. Something must be done; some courageous person must volunteer. I'm free; I'm ready; I'm willing. . . . Oh, yes, you may subscribe to my paper and keep up with the *real* truth. Three dollars will enroll you in my movement, and for $5.00 you may have a copy of my latest book."

4. *Intellectual Stagnation*

When orthodoxy says that the Bible is the only rule of faith and practice, the fundamentalist promptly concludes that everything worth knowing is in the Bible. The result is a withdrawal from the dialogue of man as man. Nothing can be learned from general wisdom, says the fundamentalist, for the natural man is wrong in starting point, method, and conclusion. When the natural man says, "This is a rose," he means "This is a not-made-by-the-triune-God rose." Everything he says is blasphemy.

It is *non-sequitur* reasoning of this sort which places fundamentalism at the extreme right in the theological spectrum. Classical orthodoxy says that God is revealed in general as well as in special revelation. The Bible *completes* the witness of God in nature; it does not negate it.

Since the fundamentalist belittles the value of general wisdom, he is often content with an educational system that substitutes piety for scholarship. High standards of education might tempt the students to trust in the arm of flesh. Moreover, if the students are exposed to damaging as well as to supporting evidences, their faith might be threatened. As a result, the students do not earn their right to believe, and they are filled with pride because they do not sense their deficiency.

The intellectual stagnation of fundamentalism can easily be illustrated. Knowing little about the canons of lower criticism, and less about the relation between language and culture, the fundamentalist has no norm by which to classify the relative merits of Biblical translations. As a result, he identifies the Word of God with the seventeenth-century language forms of the King James Version. Since other versions sound unfamiliar to him, he concludes that someone is tampering with the Word of God.

This stagnation explains why the fundamentalist is not disturbed by the difficulties in orthodoxy. Faithful to ideological thinking, he simply denies that there *are* any difficulties. To admit a difficulty would imply a lack of faith, and a lack of faith is sin.

5. *The Negative Ethic*

When the fundamentalist develops his ethical code, he is somewhat prompted by a quest for status in the cult. Consequently, he defines the *good* life as the *separated* life — separated, that is, from prevailing social mores. Whereas Christ was virtuous because he loved God with all his heart and his neighbor as himself, the fundamentalist is virtuous because he does not smoke, dance, or play cards. By raising a scrupulous demur over social mores, the fundamentalist can divert attention from grosser sins — anger, jealousy, hatred, gossip, lust, idleness, malice, backbiting, schism, guile, injustice, and every shade of illicit pride. This strategy places fundamentalism in the general tradition of the Donatists. Since the Donatists had not handed the Scriptures over to the Diocletian inquisitors (they were not among the traditores), they supposed they were virtuous. By accenting the sins that they did *not* have, they took an easy attitude toward the sins that they *did* have.

An anxiety for negative status betrays fundamentalism into glaring hypocrisy. For example, a fundamentalist is very certain that smoking is sinful, for smoking harms the body and it is habit-forming. Yet, reasonably equivalent objections can be raised against excessive coffee drinking. The nerves may be upset or a stomach ulcer induced, and the practice is habit-forming. But the fundamentalist conveniently ignores this parallel. An attack on smoking ensures status in the cult, while an attack on coffee drinking does not. Moreover, the fundamentalist enjoys his coffee, and plenty of it. Since medical tranquilizers soothe his nerves, he does not need to smoke.

The fundamentalist is also very certain that movie attendance is sinful, for the movie industry is a tool of Satan. But when the fundamentalist judges films on television, he uses a radically different criterion. There is a cultic reason for this shift in standards. Fundamentalists, it so happens, are afraid of one another. If a fundamentalist is seen entering a theater, he may be tattled on by a fellow fundamentalist. In this event the guilty party would " lose his testimony," i.e., his status in the cult would be threatened. But when he watches movies on television, this threat does not exist. Drawn shades keep prying eyes out. One of the unexpected blessings of television is that it lets the fundamentalist catch up on all the movies he missed on religious principles.

Fundamentalists defend the gospel, to be sure, but they sometimes act as if the gospel read, " Believe on the Lord Jesus Christ, don't smoke, don't go to movies, and above all don't use the Revised Standard Version — and you will be saved." Whenever fundamentalism encourages this sort of legalism, it falls within the general tradition of the Galatian Judaizers.

Paul says we are to " avoid quarreling, to be gentle, and to show perfect courtesy toward all men " (Titus 3:3). But the fundamentalist is often so intent on negative status that he confuses courtesy with compromise. As a result, he drives cultured people from the church. For example, if a fundamentalist receives a letter from a modernist, he may go right ahead and publish it without the writer's permission. Overly anxious to attack modernism, he neglects his own duties as a Christian gentleman. He has perfect vision to see heresy in others, but not in himself.

While we must be solicitous about *doctrine,* Scripture says that our primary business is *love*. But the fundamentalist finds the first task much more inviting than the second. Despite the severest apostolic warnings, schism in the church is often interpreted as a sign of Christian virtue. Separation promotes status in the cult; unity through love does not.

6. *The Chief End of Man*

Whereas orthodoxy says that the chief end of man is to glorify God and enjoy him forever, fundamentalism says that the chief end of man is to win souls. This conversion of final causes did not come by accident.

Lest we be misunderstood, however, let it be clearly and forcefully said that evangelism *is* an incumbency on the church. Woe to the minister who has no compassion for lost souls! If we are united with Christ's cross and resurrection, we must also be united with his tears for Jerusalem.

But when the fundamentalist elevates evangelism above other Christian tasks, or when he conceives of evangelism in terms of techniques, he is no longer true to his own presuppositions. While evangelism is a sacred duty, it is by no means our only sacred duty. We offend the whole counsel of God unless we also stir up the gifts of exposition, teaching, counseling, prophecy, edification, ecclesiastical rule, and the discerning of spirits. It is not the gift which counts, but the humility with which it is received and the manner in which its duties are carried out. A missionary to the Moslems may never see a convert; but if he is faithful, he may receive a more illustrious crown than an evangelist who enjoys a high incidence of conversions. The greatest in the Kingdom must be least in himself. And from the perspective of God this may be a humble Dorcas who knits little coats and shirts for the poor.

The fundamentalist's quest for souls is subtly interlarded with a quest for status in the cult, for the soul-winner belongs to a new high-priestly caste. He can rise in prayer meeting and discourse on his accomplishments in the Kingdom. Ordinary human kindness does not have this cash value.

Fundamentalism is also governed by a strict code of hero worship. When a notorious felon is converted, fundamentalists promptly make a celebrity out of him. He is sent into evangelism without the discipline of classical theology. This neglect inflates him with the notion that he is omnicompetent. He not only tells sinners to repent, but he stands behind the sacred desk and pronounces on science, the United Nations, and the cause of immorality in France. He egregiously offends humility and truth, but he does not know enough about humility and truth to measure his offense. He adds to general insecurity by giving dangerously simple answers to bafflingly complex questions. In so doing, he unwittingly verifies Christ's observation that " the sons of this world are wiser in their own generation than the sons of light " (Luke 16:8).

Anxiety for evangelism often betrays fundamentalism into strange inconsistencies. For example, to ensure a goodly attendance at a youth rally, the fundamentalist thinks nothing of using an " intelligent horse " for entertainment, or of adapting gospel lyrics to the rhythm of the dance floor. The majesty of God and the sanctity of the church must not impede the work of saving souls.

The fundamentalist often takes a magical attitude toward the Word of God. This attitude belittles the necessity of material righteousness in the soul-winner. Get the Word out — any manner will do — and God will see that his Word does not return void. This assumes that responsibility for arousing conviction rests solely on the written Word. But the written Word says otherwise: " Let your light so shine before men, that they may see your good works and give glory to your Father who is in heaven " (Matt. 5:16). When Jesus addressed the woman at the well, he addressed her as a gentleman would (John 4:7-26). A prophet must speak, but he must speak with compassion. Example first, then precept. Unless kindness arouses a sense of fellowship, the Word of God will not arouse a sense of conviction.

Since the task of general charity is apparently unconnected with the work of saving souls, it rates low on the scale of fundamentalism. Handing out tracts is much more important than founding a hospital. As a result, unbelievers are often more sensitive to mercy, and bear a heavier load of justice, than those who come in the name of Christ. The fundamentalist is not disturbed by this, of course, for he is busy painting " Jesus Saves " on rocks in a public park.

Scripture says there are times — many more than a fundamentalist suspects — when we must view charity as an end in itself. Since Jesus came to reverse the curse on nature, *any* act of kindness brings glory to the covenant God. The parable of the good Samaritan shows this.

But such pointed Biblical evidence does not move the fundamentalist. In the face of the most distressing social need, Christ's question " Did you feed the hungry? " means to the fundamentalist " Are you winning souls? "

7. *The Category of Irony*

The predicament of fundamentalism must be viewed through the category of irony; otherwise the base for pity and forgiveness is destroyed. Although fundamentalism is orthodoxy gone cultic, the perversion is fathered by misguided zeal, not malice. This fact should be acknowledged.

Irony is kin to humor, but it is not a direct kin. Irony is paradox brought on by a zeal that overlooks the limits that original sin places on the entire human enterprise. This oversight betrays the zealot into contradiction; for the more he presses toward his goal, the more he pursues a course that is at variance with that goal.

For example, Paul says that Christians should not be conformed to this world (Rom. 12:2). Anxious to honor this injunction, the fundamentalist takes an absolute stand against dancing. In so doing he not only outrages the natural instincts of the body, but he offends the teaching of Scripture elsewhere. Though David danced before the Lord (II Sam. 6:14), the fundamentalist will not. David was more relaxed because he feared God more than he did man. He properly understood that some things are right or wrong according to circumstances. " For everything there is a season, and a time for every matter under heaven: . . . a time to mourn, and a time to dance." (Eccl. 3:1, 4.) The fundamentalist is so intimidated by the cult that his sense of social grace has all but atrophied. Although many nations perpetuate their traditions through the dance, the fundamentalist takes a harsh and unfeeling attitude toward the institution: *all* dancing is worldly; there is no stopping point between total abstinence and night-club lust. The fundamentalist laces religion with so many negative burdens that he often deprives the man on the street of the most innocent forms of recreation. And the fundamentalist defends his negations in the name of the very Lord who came that men might have life, and that they might have it abundantly.

The fundamentalist ends in irony because he does not bring his cause to the touchstone of classical theology. He fails to see that Christ reveals the limits of human virtue as well as the justice and mercy of God. When the world rejected Christ, it rejected its own ideal. An oversight of this tragedy inspires the fundamentalist with the optimism that the existing order can be defecated by orthodox doctrine. Comforted by this illusion, he takes a cavalier attitude toward the sort of compromise that keeps society decent and orderly.

Don Quixote is the literary symbol of this irony. He threw himself into the task of knight-errantry with intoxicating zeal. But since he did not understand the limits of virtue in himself, he did not understand the limits of virtue in history. This made him impatient with the realistic expedients that kept history from converting to an iniquitous tyranny. As a result, he increased general evil by overturning existing safeguards. When he met a line of prisoners, he promptly released them. Pleased with the evil he corrected, he failed to notice the evil he created. But this contradiction did not occur to him, for he thought he enjoyed a perspective that was untinctured by pride and personal interest. He did not reckon with the extent to which the ideals of knight-errantry were enlisted in the service of self-love.

The fundamentalist is a religious knight-errant. He sallies off with the doctrinaire expectation that society would resolve all its problems if other people would only become as virtuous as he is. He entertains this illusion because he identifies *possession of the Word of God* with *possession of virtue*. Having never traced the effects of original sin in the lives of those who possess the Word of God, he does not reckon with the degree to which the canons of orthodoxy are enlisted in the service of self-love. He makes no serious allowance for either his own relative understanding of the Word of God or the moral ambiguity of his vocation. Defending the Bible is a comfortable egoistic accomplishment; battling modernists is a pleasing palliative for pride. Since the fundamentalist acknowledges the *virtue* of his stand, but not the *sin*, he invests his cause with more purity and finality than it deserves. He uses the Word of God as an instrument of self-security but not self-criticism. This is the source of his zeal and the cause of his irony.

Collateral Reading

1. The fundamentalist movement published its convictions in a series of articles and pamphlets. These documents were gathered into a series of volumes called The Fundamentals, Testimony Publishing Company (not inc.), Chicago, 1910–1915.

2. The history of fundamentalism: Cole, S. G., *The History of Fundamentalism*, R. R. Smith, New York, 1931; Furniss, Norman F., *The Fundamentalist Controversy, 1918–1931*, Yale University Press, 1954.

3. Ideological thinking in the political arena: Cowell, F. R., "A Republic and Its Natural Diseases," in *The Saturday Review*, Jan. 26, 1957; Halle, Louis J., "Strategy Versus Ideology," in *The Yale Review*, Autumn, 1956, pp. 1–21.

4. The classical creeds and the details of eschatology: Brown, J. A., "The Second Advent and the Creeds of Christendom," in *Bibliotheca Sacra*, Vol. XXIV (1867), pp. 629–651.

5. J. Gresham Machen's struggles with modernism: Machen, *Christianity and Liberalism*, Wm. B. Eerdmans Publishing Company, 1946. His struggles with the Presbyterian Church U.S.A.: Loetscher, Lefferts A., *The Broadening Church*, pp. 90–155, University of Pennsylvania, 1954; Stonehouse, Ned B., *J. Gresham Machen*, pp. 351–506, Wm. B. Eerdmans Publishing Company, 1954.

6. Ideological thinking and the art of containment: Smith, T. V., *The Ethics of Compromise*, Starr King Press, 1956. Casuistry as the meeting ground of Christian love and cultural necessity: Long, Edward LeRoy, Jr., *Conscience and Compromise*, The Westminster Press, 1954. Christian responsibility and the social dimension of evil: Zylstra, Henry, "Wordsworth and Hollywood," in *Testament of Vision*, pp. 87–90, Wm. B. Eerdmans Publishing Company, 1958.

7. The psychology of intolerance: Allport, Gordon W., *The Nature of Prejudice*, Addison-Wesley Publishing Company, Inc., 1954.

IX.

Future

If orthodoxy is willing to correct the cause of its present weakness, it may justly look to future strength. But the strength will not come by mere desire. The desire must convert to action, and at least three elements go into such action.

1. Overcome Minority Group Attitudes

The theology of orthodoxy is one of which no fair-minded individual need be ashamed, for evidences are sifted by appropriate criteria, and a sincere effort is made to honor the rights of language in Scripture. But orthodoxy tarnishes the splendor of its theology by taking on minority group attitudes. These attitudes include a compulsive necessity to be right on every question, an excessive dedication to self-interest, and a cultic refusal to enter into the wider Christian dialogue.

Orthodoxy is insecure because it neglects the majesty of its own traditions. If it would immerse itself in the great literature of the church, it would find that the cardinal doctrines of the faith have been defended by a train of pious and learned men from the first century until now. The theology of orthodoxy is the theology of the Reformers, and the theology of the Reformers is the theology of the prophets and apostles.

Orthodoxy is also insecure because it fails to practice what it preaches. Although believers are a remnant of grace, they belong to a fellowship that includes the redeemed of all ages. This fellowship is the Christian church, the body of Christ. Minority group attitudes have no place in the church, for Christians find their status in the promises of the covenant God, not in the petty alliances of human devising.

When orthodoxy recovers its fit and proper status, it will be relieved of the cultic urge to use the gospel as an ideological weapon against the natural man. The gospel does not make a believer omniscient, nor does it give him a monopoly on wisdom. The gospel answers one question: How can a sinner be just before God? General wisdom is not a threat to the gospel, because everything good traces to God. God is merciful and kind; he bestows *truth,* as well as rain and sunshine, upon the just and the unjust. Christ is the "true light that enlightens every man" (John 1:9). This bestowal should inspire feelings of joy, not resentment, in the heart of a Christian. Aristotle said many wise things about logic, Confucius many wise things about morals. When a Christian attacks general wisdom in the name of the gospel, the natural man will attack the gospel in the name of general wisdom.

2. *Bear the Mark of a True Disciple*

Although Jesus plainly says, "By this all men will know that you are my disciples, if you have love for one another" (ch. 13:35), orthodoxy often says, "By this all men will know that you are my disciples, if you defend orthodox doctrine." This shift in criteria places believers at the disposal of demonic pretense, for not only is Satan an accomplished student of Scripture, but the demons often address Jesus with language used by the angels. While doctrine illuminates the plan of salvation, the mark of a true disciple is *love,* not doctrine. Scripture teaches this with such clarity and force that only a highly developed sense of religious pride could miss it. "And if I have prophetic powers, and understand all mysteries and all knowledge, and if I have all faith, so as to remove mountains, but have not love, I am nothing." (I Cor. 13:2.) Doctrine puffs up, love edifies.

Edward Gibbon says that though the pagans derided the doctrines of the early church, they were sincerely impressed by the benevolence of the new society; for the early Christians paid more attention to the need of the distressed person than to his merit. "Humility and love," J. C. Ryle observes, "are precisely the graces which the men of the world can understand, if they do not comprehend doctrines. They are the graces about which there is no mystery, and they are within reach of all classes. The poorest and most ignorant Christian can every day find occasion for practicing love and humility." [1]

The natural man knows that love is the law of life because he is made in the image of God. He enjoys an intuition of his own spiritual dignity from the first moment of moral self-consciousness. He will call no man good who fails to give signs of receiving this dignity. If he is treated in an unkind or unjust way, the judicial sentiment is aroused within him; and this sentiment stays aroused until right moral conditions prevail. The offending party must either apologize or repent, depending on the situation. This is why Jesus names love as the mark of a true disciple. Unless the bearer of the gospel is sympathetic and kind, his auditors will be too occupied with a defense of their own dignity to hear the gospel.

Jesus prayed that his followers would be knit together with such perfect cords of love that when the world saw the church it would see an image of the Son's union with the Father. "The glory which thou hast given me I have given to them, that they may be one even as we are one, I in them and thou in me, that they may become perfectly one, so that the world may know that thou hast sent me and hast loved them even as thou hast loved me." (John 17:22-23.) In commenting on this passage, J. C. Ryle observes: "We can ask no stronger proof of the value of unity among Christians, and the sinfulness of divisions, than the great prominence which our Master assigns to the subject in this passage. How painfully true it is that in every age divisions have been the scandal of religion, and the weakness of the church of Christ! How often Christians have wasted their strength in contending against their brethren, instead of contending against sin and the devil! How repeatedly they have given occasion to the world to say, 'When you have settled your own internal differences, we will believe!'"

Just as the human body is an organism in which each part draws its life from the whole, so the church is a fellowship in which each member finds himself by losing himself. "If one member suffers, all

suffer together; if one member is honored, all rejoice together."
(I Cor. 12:26.) This is the ideal, and Scripture states it with clarity
and precision. But what does the world see when it looks at the
church? Instead of a warm fellowship where each prefers his brother
in love, it sees a knot of quarreling sects. "Once Parthians and
Medes and Elamites, Cretans and Arabians, the dwellers in Meso-
potamia, in Judea and Cappadocia, Pontus and Asia, heard the common language of the gospel with a common joy. Now they and their
modern heirs are without a common language; the joy of the great
community has been lost in the bickerings, rivalries, and misunder-
standings of divided sects. The accord of Pentecost has resolved itself
into a Babel of confused sounds; while devout men and women continue devoutly to confess, Sunday by Sunday, ' I believe in one, holy,
catholic church.' " [2] When the gospel incites a spirit of rancor among
those who claim to be its finest product, what attraction will the
gospel have to outsiders?

While the world is offended by the physical divisions in the
church, the *real* offense is the manner in which these divisions are
used as vehicles of pride and pretense. "Denominationalism in the
Christian church is such an unacknowledged hypocrisy. It is a compromise, made far too lightly, between Christianity and the world.
Yet it often regards itself as a Christian achievement and glorifies its
martyrs as bearers of the cross. It represents the accommodation of
Christianity to the caste system of human society. It carries over into
the organization of the Christian principle of brotherhood the prides
and prejudices, the privileges and prestige, as well as the humilia-
tions and abasements, the injustices and inequalities of that specious
order of high and low wherein men find the satisfaction of their
craving for vainglory. The division in the churches closely follows
the division of men into the castes of national, racial, and economic
groups." [3]

As long as sin dwells in our members, divisions in the church will
be natural and necessary; but to say that they are natural and necessary does not mean that they are desirable or good. Christian fellowship repudiates *any* separation of brother from brother in the community of faith.

If the church were to repent of its failure to show the love of God, not only would the way be opened for the creation of new ties of fellowship, but the principle of double fulfillment would be free to operate on the attitudes of the natural man. He might interpret the failures of the church in the light of his own failures. But when divisions in the church are held in pride and pretense, the natural man loses all patience.

Denominational distinctives are an index to our blindness, not our vision, for if we knew Christ as we ought, we would succeed in mediating the gospel without dividing brother from brother on the level of the local community. As Melville observes, "Heaven have mercy on us all — Presbyterians and Pagans alike — for we are all somehow dreadfully cracked about the head, and sadly need mending." The apostles went everywhere preaching the gospel, but sectarians go everywhere preaching the Episcopal view of succession, the Lutheran view of the real presence, the Baptist view of immersion, the Methodist view of holiness, and the Pentecostal view of speaking in tongues. Church history proves that denominational distinctives trace to very ambiguous evidences. They have no right to share honors with the gospel; they are adjectives, not nouns.

The difficulty, of course, is that though this is cheerfully acknowledged in the abstract, the denominations are all the while taking active steps to ensure the finality and perpetuity of their own vested interests. As a result, new walls are raised against a truly church-wide fellowship. For example, when a young seminarian appears before the committee on ordination, the decisive question is not, Do you believe the gospel and will you preach it with power and conviction? but rather, Will you support the program of the denomination? Ordination should be for the Christian ministry; denominationalism makes it an initiation into the cult.

Roman Catholicism believes that its unity transcends sectarian interests, but this is sheer pretense. Change the name "Roman Catholic" to "Italian Universal" and the sectarian interests come into full relief. The church is Italian because the seat of power is in Rome, and it is universal because the personality of the priest is divorced from the efficacy of the sacraments. Although Roman Catholicism is the oldest and largest branch of Christendom, it is as much a denomination as the German Lutheran or the African Methodist. Unity through hierarchical control is a far cry from fellowship in Christ Jesus.

But Rome at least announces its pretense. While other denominations *say* they are fallible, in practice they often act as if they believed they were infallible. Rome's pretense is not very convincing, but it is refreshingly forthright, nonetheless.

The body of Christ is a family, and in this family there are bound to be differences of temperament and taste. These differences will play an active part in defining the configurations that the church assumes when it enters the complexity and sinfulness of the social order. Denominational ties must gratify personal interests as well as the hunger and thirst for righteousness. Some believers prefer to worship God through elaborate ritual, while others prefer the simple forms of prayer, testimony, and song; and neither group has any reason to think that its access to the throne of grace is superior to the other. Even a minister of the gospel will admit that his denominational convictions often trace to evidences that are as difficult to name as they are to defend. The denomination of our childhood houses memories as well as truth.

Original sin prevents history from accepting its own ideals — including the ideal of visible Christian unity. As long as sin dwells in our members, we shall continue to express our faith along sectarian lines that are partly a refutation of that faith. But this ambiguity is merely an occasion for love to manifest its creative possibilities. Love understands why divisions in the church are simultaneously necessary and sinful. There is a *risk* in freedom, and love cheerfully accepts this risk. Parents do not conform their children to some abstract standard; nor does a gardener make all his flowers alike; for the beauty is in the variety.

3. *Return to the Classical View of the Church*

Contemporary orthodoxy is a curious blend of classical and cultic elements, for whereas it claims to be true to general Biblical doctrine, it defends a separatist view of the church. Behind this inconsistency is the familiar error of thinking that possession of truth is the same thing as possession of virtue. As long as orthodoxy is comforted by this error, it imagines that it is sufficiently virtuous to decide who are, and who are not, members of the church. And once the nature of church membership is decided, it is only a matter of mechanics to decide the nature of the church itself. Since only defenders of orthodoxy are fit members of the church (they alone are virtuous), the presence or absence of the church is measured by the presence or absence of such members. This is how the separatist mentality operates. When the Bible says, "Therefore come out from them, and be separate from them, says the Lord, and touch nothing unclean" (II Cor. 6:17), the separatist puts one construction on this counsel: he must physically withdraw from any communion that is not purely orthodox. An endless proliferation results.

Unless contemporary orthodoxy learns to distinguish between the classical and cultic elements in its own theology, it may destroy itself in its zeal to preserve itself. The separatist operates on a principle that, if carried out consistently, would invalidate Christian theology at *every* point; for if we do not need the Word of God when defining the nature of the church, why do we need it when we define the nature of anything else? The separatist reverses right procedure by substituting pious speculation for the normative testimony of Christ and the apostles.

The following principles define orthodoxy's traditional attitude toward existing denominations. And if it should seem that orthodoxy is more concerned with separation than it is with union, one very important observation must be borne in mind: namely, that it is only by clarifying the legitimate conditions of separation that we can define the legitimate possibilities of union.

First: All other things being equal, a Christian should remain in the fellowship that gave him spiritual birth. A filial obligation requires this. For example, Paul did not minister to the Gentiles until he had preached the gospel to his fellow Jews; and in doing so, he followed the express example of Jesus Christ. "He came to his own home, and his own people received him not." (John 1:11.)

Secondly: A Christian should judge the claims of a church by

its official creed or confession, not by the lives of its members. False
priests in the Temple did not make the Temple any less the house
of God; nor did the apostasy of Judas make the apostolic college
any less a perfect instrument of God's will. When believers are unfaithful or immoral, they must be disciplined; but the nature of the
church is not disturbed by their perfidy. "When we affirm the pure
ministry of the word, and pure order in the celebration of the sacraments, to be a sufficient pledge and earnest, that we may safely embrace the society in which both these are found, as a true church, we
carry the observation to this point, that such a society should never
be rejected as long as it continues in those things, although in
other respects it may be chargeable with many faults. It is possible,
moreover, that some fault may insinuate itself into the preaching of
the doctrine, or the administration of the sacraments, which ought
not to alienate us from its communion." [4]

In order that the force of this might be felt, the following questions are raised. These questions can help a searching mind to decide whether a denomination may rightfully be called a church.

a. *Is the gospel taught in the creed or confession?* A denomination
is not part of the church if its creed or confession is out of harmony
with the system of theology taught in Romans and Galatians. The
gospel is the good news that God offers pardon through Jesus Christ,
the blessing of the Abrahamic covenant; and Romans and Galatians are the only places where this teaching is developed in systematic, didactic form. Therefore, if a denomination officially rejects the gospel, it forfeits its right to be called a church.

b. *Is the gospel free?* It is not enough that the gospel be in the
creed or confession. If a denomination forbids the preaching of the
gospel, the result is the same as not having the gospel. Luther encountered this anomaly in the Roman Church, for his right to preach
the gospel was placed under papal interdict.

It is here, however, that the separatist tends to go astray. He confuses freedom to preach the gospel with whether the gospel, in fact,
is being preached. He does not realize that a denomination may be
part of the Christian church, even though there are many — clergy
and others — who not only reject the gospel, but who take active

steps to preach a false gospel. The church exists when the gospel is in the creed or confession, on the one hand, and when believers are free to preach the gospel, on the other. Wicked members do *not* make the church apostate. " Among the Corinthians, more than a few had gone astray, and the infection had seized almost the whole society; there was not only one species of sin, but many; and they were not trivial faults, but dreadful crimes; and there was not only a corruption of morals, but of doctrine. In this case, what is the conduct of the holy apostle, the organ of the heavenly Spirit, by whose testimony the church stands or falls? Does he seek to separate from them? Does he reject them from the Kingdom of Christ? Does he strike them with the thunderbolt of the severest anathema? He not only does none of these things, but, on the contrary, acknowledges and speaks of them as a church of Christ and a society of saints." [5]

c. *Is the Christian free to protest against abuses?* Since the visible church is formed of sinners, a believer may occasionally be drawn into federal decisions that offend either virtue or truth. In such situations a believer delivers his conscience by registering a sincere and forceful protest through legitimate channels. For example, Joseph of Arimathea was a member of the council that condemned Christ; but since he " had not consented to their purpose and deed " (Luke 23: 51), Scripture calls him a good and righteous man. This illustrates the principle by which a prudent believer governs his conduct. He must speak against abuses with power and grace. And if his words fail to effect a change, he must patiently wait for a new opportunity to speak. He may *not* take the law into his own hands by provoking schism, for final judgment belongs to God, not man. " To pious and peaceable persons he [Augustine] gives this advice: that they should correct in mercy whatever they can; that what they cannot, they should patiently bear, and affectionately lament, till God either reform or correct it, or, at the harvest, root up the tares and sift out the chaff. All pious persons should study to fortify themselves with these counsels, lest, while they consider themselves as valiant and strenuous defenders of righteousness, they depart from the Kingdom of Heaven, which is the only Kingdom of righteousness. For since it is the will of God that the communion of his church should be maintained in this external society, those who, from an aversion of wicked men, destroy the token of that society, enter on a course in which they are in great danger of falling from the communion of the saints." [6]

Here, again, the separatist tends to go astray. He thinks that if he remains in a fellowship that is not purely orthodox, he compromises his faith. He becomes so intent on separating from heretics that his zeal becomes the norm by which he decides the nature of the church. *He forgets that the nature of the church, like the nature of anything else in the theological encyclopedia, is decided by the testimony of Christ and the apostles, not by the testimony of separatists.* The evidence is plain, and no amount of piety can change a line of it: Christ and the apostles did *not* decide the nature of the church by the presence or absence of heretics in the church. " Now, what kind of an age was that of Christ and the apostles? Yet the desperate impiety of the Pharisees, and the dissolute lives every where led by the people, could not prevent *them* from using the same sacrifices, and assembling in the same temple with others, for the public exercises of religion. How did this happen, but from a knowledge that the society of the wicked could not contaminate those who with pure consciences united with them in the same solemnities? If any one pay no deference to the prophets and apostles, let him at least acquiesce in the authority of Christ. Cyprian has excellently remarked: ' Although tares, or impure vessels, are found in the church, yet this is not a reason why we should withdraw from it. It only behooves us to labor that we may be the wheat, and to use our utmost endeavors and exertions, that we may be vessels of gold or of silver. But to break in pieces the vessels of earth belongs to the Lord alone, to whom a rod of iron is also given. Nor let any one arrogate to himself what is exclusively the province of the Son of God, by pretending to fan the floor, clear away the chaff, and separate all the tares by the judgment of man. This is proud obstinacy and sacrilegious presumption, originating in a corrupt frenzy.' " [7]

Thirdly: Separation from an existing denomination is justifiable on only two criteria.

a. *Eviction.* If a believer is evicted — as the apostles were by the

Jews, and as the Reformers were by Rome — a new fellowship must be formed. This is obvious. But the necessity must trace to ineptness among those who initiate the action, not among those who suffer it. To force a new fellowship through either pride, imprudence, or insubordination, is hardly a work of grace.

b. *Apostasy*. If a denomination removes the gospel from its creed or confession, or if it leaves the gospel but removes the believer's right to preach it, the believer may justly conclude that the denomination is apostate. It is no longer part of the church; a new fellowship must be formed.

But before a believer takes a settled attitude one way or another, he must bring his convictions to the touchstone: he must seek the counsel of the brethren and the wisdom of classical theology. A spirit of divisiveness is not prompted by the Holy Spirit, for love is the law of life, and love remains unsatisfied until *all* who form the body of Christ are united in one sacred fellowship.

COLLATERAL READING

1. The classical inquiry into the criteria of heresy: Taylor, Jeremy, *A Discourse of the Liberty of Prophesying*. Contemporary inquiry: Hall, Alfred, " Who Is Orthodox? " in *The Hibbert Journal*, Vol. LII (1953), pp. 156–159; Turner, H. E. W., *The Pattern of Christian Truth*, A. R. Mowbray & Co., Ltd., London, 1954.

2. The classical conversation on toleration: Locke, John, *Four Letters Concerning Toleration;* Mill, John Stuart, *On Liberty*, Ch. II; Milton, John, *Areopagitica*. Contemporary conversation: Gilson, Etienne, *Dogmatism and Tolerance*, Rutgers University Press, 1952; Jordan, W. K., *The Development of Religious Toleration in England*, Harvard University Press, 1936; Miller, Perry, *et al.*, *Religion and Freedom of Thought*, Doubleday & Co., Inc., 1954.

3. The doctrine of the church: Bannerman, D. Douglas, *The Scripture Doctrine of the Church*, T. & T. Clark, Edinburgh, 1887; Binnie, William, *The Church*, T. & T. Clark, Edinburgh, n.d.; Cunningham, William, *Discussions on Church Principles*, T. & T. Clark, Edinburgh, 1863; Hodge, Charles, *Discussions in Church Polity*, Charles Scribner's Sons, 1878; Oman, John, " Church," in

Hastings, James (ed.), *Encyclopaedia of Religion and Ethics,* 13 vols., T. & T. Clark, Edinburgh, 1910; Simpson, W. J. Sparrow, *The Catholic Conception of the Church,* Robert Scott, London, 1914; Thomas, W. H. Griffith, *The Principles of Theology,* pp. 265–290, Longmans, Green & Co., Inc., 1930. When reading these sources, however, due allowance must be made for covert denominational interests.

4. Fellowship, organization, and the church: Brunner, Emil, *The Misunderstanding of the Church,* The Westminster Press, 1953. Although Brunner overstates his case, he nicely challenges the tendency to view the church as an organization.

X.

Conclusion

ORTHODOXY does not have all the answers; nor does it always ask the right questions. And when it gives the right answers to the right questions, it often corrupts its claims with bad manners.

But beneath these outer garments is the warm flesh of Christian truth: the truth that love is the law of life; that all men are sinners; that Christ bore the penalty of sin; that repentant sinners are clothed with the righteousness of Christ; that Christ is confronted in and through the written Word; and that the written Word is consistent with itself and consistent with the things signified.

We have defined orthodoxy as " that branch of Christendom which limits the ground of religious authority to the Bible." The testimony of Christ is normative for the church, and included in this testimony is the assurance that the written Word is inspired of God, and that it has the force of law.

1. *Literalism*

Orthodoxy is often branded as literalism. The charge is that orthodoxy defends the plenary inspiration of the Bible, even though destructive criticism has ostensibly demolished this doctrine. But it is instructive to note that the critics seldom give a precise definition of literalism; nor do they go on to tell what *they* mean by the Bible as the Word of God. If orthodoxy neglects destructive criticism out of a respect for the testimony of Christ, the critics neglect the testimony of Christ out of a respect for destructive criticism. Not only is the neglect mutual, but it is by no means clear that the neglect of the critics is more praiseworthy, let alone more Christian, than that of orthodoxy.

If we nullify the testimony of Christ at one point, we operate on a principle that leaves the mind free to nullify this testimony at all points. In this case we have little reason to believe that our hope rests on divinely appointed evidences — not even our hope that God sent his Son to be the Savior of the world. The evidences that support the plan of salvation are precisely the same in quantity and quality as those which support the plenary inspiration of the Bible.

If orthodoxy is literalistic because it honors the rights of language in Scripture, it is in very good company, for Christ and the apostles approach the text in precisely the same manner. Critical reinterpretation may relieve faith of the scandal of plenary inspiration, but it also relieves faith of the scandal of the cross. Tested by the canons of science and philosophy, the doctrine of justification fares no better than the doctrine of plenary inspiration.

When the gospel is absorbed into a world system, the minister can no longer stand behind the sacred desk and cry, " Thus says the Lord! " And when the voice of the prophet is silenced, let " Ichabod " be written over the church: the glory has departed.

The cause of destructive criticism cannot be rescued by contending that revelation is personal encounter with Christ, and that this encounter is valid whether or not the Bible is inspired. Not only is the contention void of proof, but it reduces Christian commitment to a variety of religious experience. By no analysis of personal confrontation could we discover that God made a covenant with Abraham, and that Jesus Christ is the blessing of this covenant. Only propositional revelation can clarify the state of a sinner before a holy God.

Christ taught that the plan of salvation was mediated to the church through the office of inspired prophets and apostles. If we reject this office, we forfeit the norm by which the limits of valid confrontation are decided. In this case the religious experience of an animist has the same rights as that of a Christian, for neither the animist nor the Christian has any proof that his faith terminates in the mind of God. Religion becomes an exercise in personal feeling.

2. *Fundamentalism*

Critics also brand orthodoxy as fundamentalism, but in doing so they act in bad taste. Not only is it unfair to identify a position with its worst elements, but the critics of fundamentalism often manifest the very attitudes that they are trying to expose. The mentality of fundamentalism is by no means an exclusive property of orthodoxy. Its attitudes are found in *every* branch of Christendom: the quest for negative status, the elevation of minor issues to a place of major importance, the use of social mores as a norm of virtue, the toleration of one's own prejudice but not the prejudice of others, the confusion of the church with a denomination, and the avoidance of prophetic scrutiny by using the Word of God as an instrument of self-security but not self-criticism.

The mentality of fundamentalism comes into being whenever a believer is unwilling to trace the effects of original sin in his own life. And where is the believer who is wholly delivered from this habit? This is why no one understands fundamentalism until he understands the degree to which he himself is tinctured by the attitudes of fundamentalism.

3. *The Sum of the Matter*

Critics have not performed their full task until they leave the externals of orthodoxy and probe into the heart of the system itself. And once this nobler task has been executed, the critics may discover that orthodoxy is a worthy Christian option. In any case, the problems of orthodoxy are common to all who try to discover the essence of Christianity and to live by its precepts.

In the sweep of history it may turn out that orthodoxy will fail in its vocation. But in this event it should be observed that it is orthodoxy, not the gospel, which has failed. The Word of God is *not* voided by the frailties of those who come in the name of the Word of God. " Heaven and earth will pass away, but my words will not pass away." (Luke 21:33.)

Notes

I. Foundations

1. Herman Bavinck, *Our Reasonable Faith,* p. 76. Wm. B. Eerdmans Publishing Company, 1956.
2. *Ibid.,* p. 81.
3. James Orr, *Revelation and Inspiration,* p. 22. Wm. B. Eerdmans Publishing Company, 1953.
4. John Calvin, *Institutes,* II. xi. 2.
5. Charles Hodge, *Commentary on the Epistle to the Romans,* p. 16. Wm. B. Eerdmans Publishing Company, 1950.

II. Faith

1. Thomas Aquinas, *Summa Theologica,* Second Part of the Second Part, Q. 1, Art. 5.
2. Abraham Kuyper, *Principles of Sacred Theology,* p. 131. Wm. B. Eerdmans Publishing Company, 1954.
3. James Buchanan, *The Office and Work of the Holy Spirit,* p. 194. John Johnstone, Edinburgh, 1842.
4. Hodge, *Commentary on the Epistle to the Romans,* p. 130.
5. Calvin, *Institutes,* III. ii. 17.

III. Authority

1. Kuyper, *Principles of Sacred Theology,* p. 551.
2. William Lee, *The Inspiration of Holy Scripture* (3d ed.), p. 102. Hodges, Smith & Company, Dublin, 1864.

3. Kuyper, *Principles of Sacred Theology,* pp. 435–436.

4. B. B. Warfield, *The Inspiration and Authority of the Bible,* pp. 138–140. The Presbyterian and Reformed Publishing Company, 1948.

5. Kuyper, *Principles of Sacred Theology,* p. 441.

6. William G. T. Shedd, *Dogmatic Theology,* Vol. I, p. 137. Zondervan Publishing House, n.d.

7. Lee, *op. cit.,* p. 70.

8. Kuyper, *Principles of Sacred Theology,* p. 430.

9. *Ibid.,* pp. 455–457.

10. *Ibid.,* p. 446.

11. Lee, *op. cit.,* pp. 262–263.

12. Robert S. Candlish, *Reason and Revelation,* p. 36. Thomas Nelson & Sons, Ltd., London, 1859.

13. Warfield, *The Inspiration and Authority of the Bible,* pp. 208–210.

14. *Ibid.,* p. 218.

15. Shedd, *op. cit.,* p. 143.

16. William Cunningham, *Theological Lectures,* pp. 414–415. Robert Carter & Brothers, 1878.

17. Kuyper, *Principles of Sacred Theology,* p. 465.

18. Warfield, *The Inspiration and Authority of the Bible,* p. 163.

19. *Ibid.,* pp. 164–165.

20. Cunningham, *Theological Lectures,* pp. 442–443 (italics mine).

21. *Ibid.,* pp. 425–428 (italics mine).

22. Warfield, *The Inspiration and Authority of the Bible,* pp. 415–416.

23. Cunningham, *Theological Lectures,* p. 441.

24. Kuyper, *Principles of Sacred Theology,* pp. 413–414.

IV. HERMENEUTICS

1. Orr, *Revelation and Inspiration,* pp. 102–103.

2. *Ibid.,* pp. 176–177.

3. Calvin, *Institutes,* II. xi. 12.

4. Richard Whately, *A View of the Scripture Revelations Concerning a Future State* (10th ed.), pp. 137–138. Longmans, Green & Co. Ltd., London, 1877.

5. *Ibid.,* pp. 149–150.

6. Matthew Henry, *A Commentary on the Holy Bible,* Ex. 22:18.

7. Richard Baxter, *The Reasons of the Christian Religion,* II, 3.

8. Calvin, *Institutes,* II. xi. 3.

9. *Ibid.,* III. xvi. 1.

10. John Owen, *Works* (Wm. Goold, ed.), Vol. V, pp. 384–385. T. & T. Clark, Edinburgh, 1862.

11. Whately, *op. cit.,* pp. 163–164.

V. Theology

1. F. W. Farrar, *The Life and Work of St. Paul,* pp. 451–452. E. P. Dutton & Co., Inc., 1880.

2. Hodge, *Commentary on the Epistle to the Romans,* p. 223.

3. *Ibid.,* p. 226.

4. William Cunningham, *Historical Theology,* Vol. II, p. 46. T. & T. Clark, Edinburgh, 1864.

5. Calvin, *Institutes,* II. xvi. 10.

6. James Buchanan, *The Doctrine of Justification,* p. 17. Baker Book House, 1955.

7. Cunningham, *Historical Theology,* pp. 40–41.

8. Horatius Bonar, *God's Way of Holiness,* pp. 121–122. Robert Carter & Brothers, 1870.

9. Hodge, *Commentary on the Epistle to the Romans,* p. 184.

10. *Ibid.,* p. 156.

11. Charles Hodge, *Essays and Reviews,* p. 59. Robert Carter & Brothers, 1879.

12. Owen, *Works* (Wm. Goold, ed.), Vol. III, p. 369.

13. Abraham Kuyper, *The Work of the Holy Spirit,* p. 459. Wm. B. Eerdmans Publishing Company, 1946.

14. Hodge, *Commentary on the Epistle to the Romans,* p. 232.

15. Bonar, *op. cit.,* pp. 247–248.

16. Hodge, *Commentary on the Epistle to the Romans,* p. 234.

17. *Ibid.,* p. 231.

18. Buchanan, *The Office and Work of the Holy Spirit,* pp. 207–208.

19. Hodge, *Commentary on the Epistle to the Romans,* pp. 136–137.

20. Kuyper, *The Work of the Holy Spirit,* p. 441.

VI. Proof

1. David Hume, *An Inquiry Concerning the Human Understanding,* Section 10, Part 2.

2. Hodge, *Commentary on the Epistle to the Romans,* p. 127.

3. James Orr, *Revelation and Inspiration,* pp. 88–89.

VII. DIFFICULTIES

1. John Calvin, *Commentary on Genesis,* 1:6, 15, 16. Wm. B. Eerdmans Publishing Company, 1948.

2. James Orr, *God's Image in Man,* p. 88. Wm. B. Eerdmans Publishing Company, 1948.

3. Patrick Fairbairn, *The Revelation of Law in Scripture,* p. 13. Zondervan Publishing House, 1957.

4. Orr, *God's Image in Man,* pp. 45–46.

5. *Ibid.,* p. 140.

6. B. B. Warfield, *Biblical and Theological Studies,* pp. 240–241. The Presbyterian and Reformed Publishing Company, 1952.

7. Robert S. Candlish, *Reason and Revelation,* p. 43.

8. James Orr, *The Bible Under Trial,* pp. 9–10. Marshall Brothers, London, 1907.

9. B. B. Warfield, " Professor Henry Preserved Smith on Inspiration," *The Presbyterian and Reformed Review,* Vol. V (1894), pp. 652–653.

10. Warfield, *The Inspiration and Authority of the Bible,* p. 420.

11. *Ibid.,* pp. 119–120.

12. Orr, *Revelation and Inspiration,* pp. 217–218.

13. *Ibid.,* pp. 197–198.

14. B. B. Warfield, " Reviews of Recent Theological Literature," *The Presbyterian and Reformed Review,* Vol. IV (1893), p. 499.

15. Orr, *Revelation and Inspiration,* p. 200.

16. Henry Preserved Smith, *Inspiration and Inerrancy: A History and a Defense,* p. 270. Robert Clarke & Company, 1893.

17. *The Princeton Review,* Vol. XXIX (1857), p. 685.

18. Smith, *op. cit.,* p. 270.

19. *Ibid.,* pp. 124–125.

20. Warfield, " Reviews of Recent Theological Literature," *The Presbyterian and Reformed Review,* Vol. IV (1893), p. 499.

21. Warfield, *The Inspiration and Authority of the Bible,* p. 226.

22. Warfield, " Professor Henry Preserved Smith on Inspiration," *The Presbyterian and Reformed Review,* Vol. V (1894), p. 650.

23. *Ibid.,* p. 646.

24. Henry, *A Commentary on the Holy Bible,* I Chron. 8:1-32.

25. Orr, *Revelation and Inspiration,* pp. 163–165.

26. A. A. Hodge and B. B. Warfield, " Inspiration," *The Presbyterian Review,* Vol. II (1881), p. 231.

27. James Bannerman, *Inspiration,* p. 557. T. & T. Clark, Edinburgh, 1865.

28. C. H. Waller, " The Authoritative Inspiration of Holy Scripture," *Fairbairn's Imperial Standard Bible Encyclopedia,* I, lix-lx. Zondervan Publishing House, 1957.

VIII. Perils

1. Calvin, *Institutes,* IV. i. 18.

2. Richard Whately, *A View of the Scripture Revelations Concerning a Future State,* pp. 154–155.

IX. Future

1. J. C. Ryle, *Expository Thoughts on the Gospels: St. John,* Vol. II, p. 238. Zondervan Publishing House, n.d.

2. H. Richard Niebuhr, *The Social Sources of Denominationalism,* p. 11. The Shoe String Press, 1954. (Hamden, Conn.)

3. *Ibid.,* p. 6.

4. Calvin, *Institutes,* IV. i. 12.

5. *Ibid.,* IV. i. 14.

6. *Ibid.,* IV. i. 16.

7. *Ibid.,* IV. i. 19.

A Bibliography of General Theological Sources

1. The ecumenical creeds of Christendom: The Apostles' Creed; The Nicene Creed; The Creed of Chalcedon; The Athanasian Creed; The Creed of the Sixth Ecumenical Council Against the Monothelites.

2. The standards of Greek and Eastern Orthodoxy: The Orthodox Confession of the Eastern Church; The Confession of Dositheus; The Longer Catechism of the Russian Church; John of Damascus, *An Exposition of the Orthodox Faith.*

3. The standards of Roman Catholicism: The Canons and Dogmatic Decrees of the Council of Trent; The Profession of the Tridentine Faith; Thomas Aquinas, *Summa Contra Gentiles* and *Summa Theologica;* Bellarmine, Robert, *Disputationum de Controversiis Christianae Fidei Adversus Haereticos,* Romae, ex Typographia Bonarum Artium, 1832–1840.

4. The standards of Lutheranism: The Augsburg Confession; Luther's Catechism; The Formula of Concord; The Saxon Visitation Articles; Luther, Martin, *Primary Works,* Hodder & Stoughton, London, 1896; Melanchthon, Philipp, *Loci Communes,* Meador Publishing Company, 1944.

5. The standards of the Reformed tradition: The Heidelberg Catechism; The Canons of the Synod of Dort; The Westminster Confession of Faith; The Westminster Shorter Catechism; Calvin, John, *Institutes of the Christian Religion.*

6. The standards of Anglicanism: The Thirty-nine Articles of the Church of England; The Anglican Catechism; Hooker, Richard, *Of the Laws of Ecclesiastical Polity.*

7. The standards of Arminianism: The Arminian Articles; Arminius, Jacobus, *Writings,* Baker Book House, 1956; Watson, Richard, *Theological Institutes,* Wesleyan-Methodist Book-Room, London, 7th edition, 1823.

Indexes

SCRIPTURE REFERENCES

NAMES AND TOPICS